essays
in
design

ESSAYS IN DESIGN

j christopher jones

john wiley & sons ltd
chichester new york brisbane toronto singapore

218434

British Library Cataloguing in Publication Data:

Jones, J Christopher
  Essays in design
  1. Design
  I. Title
  745.4   NK1510
  ISBN 0 471 90297 7

Printed in Great Britain

Human plurality, the basic condition of both action and speech,
has the twofold character of equality and distinction. If men
were not equal, they could neither understand each other and
those who came before them nor plan for the future and forsee
the needs of those who will come after them. If men were not
distinct, each human being distinguished from any other who is,
was, or ever will be, they would need neither speech nor action
to make themselves understood. Signs and sounds to communicate
immediate, identical needs and wants would be enough.

Hannah Arendt
The Human Condition

A THOUGHT REVOLVED

This title, and those of the other sections, were taken from
The Collected Poems of Wallace Stevens, Faber and Faber, 1955.
The poems from which they come were selected by chance process
using random numbers to pick a page and a position on it and
then choosing a title or subtitle from the poem that had been
selected. Having arrived at the titles in this indirect way
I am not sure what they mean or how they may be seen to relate
to the essays to which they have become names. Like our own
names, or those of apples, of musical groups, of many common
things, we are inside them. Not that we own them. My apologies, and thanks, to the memory of Wallace Stevens.

contents

preface : ix

acknowledgements : xii

A THOUGHT REVOLVED

love, hate and architecture : 3

how my thoughts about design methods have changed during
the years: 13

now we are numerous : 29

beyond rationalism : 37

principles in design : 73

2   THE WORLD WITHOUT IMAGINATION

St Ives by chance : 85

composing by chance : 105

some reflections on chance : 111

designing designing : 125

3   IT MUST GIVE PLEASURE

opus one, number two : 147

"......in the dimension of Time." : 169

continuous design and redesign : 191

things : 219

4   THINGS OF AUGUST

is designing a response to the whole of life? : 243

35 wishes : 257

voices at the conference conference : 277

the design of modern life : 303

Utopia and Numeroso : 327

ILLUSTRATIONS

On waking, Salzberg, 1969 : ii
Visual poem by Edwin Schlossberg, Blacksburg, Virginia, 1974 : xi
Visual poem by Edwin Schlossberg, Chester, Massachusetts, 1974 : xv
Automatic carpark, Austin, Texas, 1974 : 2
Root from street excavation, Zurich, 1982 : 12
Jones family shopping, London, 1975? : 28
Self-portrait, Blacksburg, Virgina, 1974 : 35
Airport, Roanoake, Virginia, 1974 : 36
View from Holland Park, London, 1976? : 71
Grass, Zurich street, 1982 : 72
Sugar from a cafe, Zurich, 1982 : 81
Cartop in desert, Arcosanti, Arizona, 1974 : 84
Steel ring from street excavation, Zurich, 1982 : 103
Metal turning, Zurich street, 1982 : 104
Blackberry leaves, Hampstead Heath, London, 1982 : 110
Metal foil, Zurich street, 1982 : 123
Piano keys, Chester, Massachusetts, 1976? : 124
Street debris, Zurich, 1982 : 143
Plastic strap, Zurich street, 1982 : 146
Nail, Zurich street, 1982 : 168
Letter shapes, copied from hairs in rag paper by Joel Fisher,
    1978 : 190
Label, Spitalfields market, London, 1982 : 217
T-shirt, chance location in house, London, 1982 : 218
Radio transmission towers, London, 1977? : 239
Ruled paper, London, 1983 : 242
Feather, Zurich street, 1982 : 256
Truck maintenance, Kilburn, London, 1976? : 275
Lawn sprays, Austin, Texas, 1974 : 276
Holland Park, London, 1976? : 302
Cows, barbed wire and prehistoric stones, Avebury, England,
    1976? : 326
On waking, Chester, Massachusetts, 1976? : 336

other illustrations, not listed, are described within the essays
to which they belong.

preface

What has become of design?

As I sit here on a Sunday afternoon looking at the titles of these
essays and wondering what they have in common I'm struck by the
extent to which the notion of design has changed.

Alongside the old idea of design as the drawing of objects that
are then to be built or manufactured there are many new ideas
of what it is, all very different:

designing as the process of devising not individual products
but whole systems or environments such as airports, transport-
ation, hypermarkets, educational curricula, broadcasting
schedules, welfare schemes, banking systems, computer networks;

design as participation, the involvement of the public in the
decision-making process;

design as creativity, which is supposed to be potentially
present in everyone;

design as an educational discipline that unites arts and sciences
and perhaps goes further than either;

and now the idea of designing WITHOUT A PRODUCT, as a process
or way of living in itself......(a way out of consumerism?)

I suppose there are other views too but these are enough to let
one see how quickly the notion has been changing and how far-
reaching are its newer implications.

In my earlier book I defined design as the initiation of change
in man-made things. Looking now at that definition I still like
the emphasis on change but not the assumption that design is
limited to the thinking of a few on behalf of many. Nor do I
like the assumption that it is to do with change in things but
not in ourselves. In my re-thinkings of the nature of design in
these pages I have moved far from the picture of 'it' as the
specialised activity of paid experts who shape the physical and
abstract forms of industrial life which we all as consumers accept

x

or adapt to. That notion cannot possibly last for ever – it's
too limiting, too insensitive to the reactions it provokes. It's
too inert. Designing, if it is to survive as an activity through
which we transform our lives, on earth, and beyond, has itself to
be redesigned, continuously. As do all the other false stabilities,
ideas of order, which we inherit or construct, as stepping-stones,
no more, useful as they may be in the moment. The turning of
creative activity upon itself, attempting to change its nature,
our own, is to me the most surprising, the most promising, of
the changes to be noticed now, not only in design but as a general
tendency:

   the science-of-science;

   learning-how-to-learn;

   the technology of assessing technology;

   'the composer as listener' (in the music of John Cage and
   other modern composers, poets, artists);

   the theory of autopoiesis (theory that includes or accounts
   for the theorist);

   the think-tank;

   the self-development movement;

what else? I see these as the turning of the objective and outward tradition of Western progress inwards towards itself as we
try to correct the by-now bad effects of having looked outwardly
for centuries......

It's time to look in the mirror as well as through the window.
Soon it may be time to leave home. But first, a better picture
of ourselves.

August, 1982

acknowledgements

These essays would not have been written but for the invitations
of the persons mentioned at the start of each. They would not
have taken the forms that they have but for what I've learnt
from the works of John Cage, Edwin Schlossberg and others whose
example may be evident in the text.

Previous publication of the essays, sources of the quotations,
and acknowledgements of permissions to republish here, are
indicated in the notes or references attached to each essay.
The sources of the opening quotation, and those before each
section-title are:

> page v
> Hannah Arendt, The Human Condition, University of Chicago
> Press, Chicago & London, 1958, pages 175-6.

> page xvi
> Annetta Pedretti, The Cybernetics of Language, Princelet
> Editions, London & Zurich, 1981, page 87.

> page 82
> John Cage, Empty Words, Writings '73-'78, Wesleyan University
> Press, Middletown, Connecticut, 1979, page 61. This quotation
> is of fragments of the writings of Henry David Thoreau
> recomposed as music to be spoken aloud.

> page 144
> Edwin Schlossberg, For My Father, in About Bateson, Essays
> on Gregory Bateson, edited by John Brockman, E P Dutton,
> New York, N Y, 1977, pages 146-7.

> page 240
> Gertrude Stein, Mrs. Reynolds and Five Earlier Novelettes,
> Yale University Press, Yale, Massachusetts, 1952, reprinted
> by Books for Libraries Press, New York, N Y, 1969, pages 242-3.

The visual poems on pages xi and xv are by Edwin Schlossberg and
are reproduced with his permission. The letter shapes on page
190 were copied from the accidental shapes of hairs in rag paper
by Joel Fisher and are reproduced with his permission. The
photographs are from colour slides I made in the last ten years
or so and the xerox pictures are of objects I found at chance-
locations in Zurich and London. The process of selecting and
positioning the quotations and illustrations is described on
pages 108-9. The choosing of the section titles is described on
page vi.

The cover was designed by Daniel Weil and much of the text was
retyped by Charlie Boxer. The book would not have appeared but
for the encouragement and help of the staff of John Wiley & Sons.

The essays were written between 1971 and 1981.

WE RETURN FROM ANGLE TO CENTER SUBSTANCE CHANGES

A complementarity arises where, in the act of distinction, a whole
is severed. It is perceived as a complementarity where we perceive
the whole severed by our distinction. Aspects distinguished are
perceived as distinct where the act of drawing the distinction is
itself passed over in silence. The distinction invoked between two
aspects of a whole is brought into question where the act of dist-
inguishing them is perceived.

Annetta Pedretti
The Cybernetics of Language

1

A THOUGHT REVOLVED

love, hate and architecture

or what is a method?

memories of a seminar in Bologna

This was written as an article for the architectural journal
Zodiac, of Milan, in March 1973. The journal, which was edited
by Maria Bottero, ceased before the article could be published.

When Maria Bottero asked for my opinions of "scientific"
design methods as a way of "controlling the environment" my
first thought was to refuse. My view of designing is deliberately unscientific and I hate the idea of controlling
anything, even a hostile environment. Science implies
sticking to what already exists and control implies lack of
respect for something. Design implies respect for the new.
However, Maria reminded me also of the happy times we both
had at a seminar on design methods in Bologna* and I realised
that it is human experience and not abstract theories that
should decide what we do.

So, having agreed to write an article, I tried to find something to say that would include both experience and theory.
What resulted is an imaginary conversation.............The
conversation is one of questions and answers. It is inspired
by the notes I made while waiting for the translators to say
what I had just said at the Bologna seminar. It is not,
however, a true record of what was said, but a mixture of the
thoughts, doubts and memories that I now have of the occasion.

My apologies to those who were present: they will realise how
far this imagined conversation is from what actually happened.

*At the Institute of Architecture and Urban Planning in the
Faculty of Engineering at the University of Bologna in 1971.

Q. What is the relationship between design methods and technology?

A. I don't feel that the relationship between methods and technology is the right question. Maybe its more helpful to regard methods not as things but as relationships, or as ways of enabling things to get into better relationship with each other. To me designing is a way of improving relations between objects and people. It is important that this relationship is two-way. Winston Churchill put it very well when he said "We shape our houses and our houses shape us". With the wrong methods one or both of these two life-shaping connections is missing. This two-way relationship should be one of complementarity such as exists between seasons, lovers, enemies, colours or between the observer and the observed (the uncertainty principle).

I guess that the big fault of industrial life is that relationships operate in only one direction but should operate in two. We now expect technical change to cause social change as a matter of course but attempts to make social change influence technology are still thought of as revolutionary. They should be normal. If they were, both "technology" and "society" should cease to be fixed objects or false gods. They would become ever changing elements of a new kind of living, something more like music or dancing and less like painting or sculpture.

Q. Is designing a process of mystifying or clarifying?

A. If a design method hides the real issues, it mystifies; if it reveals them, it clarifies. In planning a new university the methodologist, or analyst, could either accept or ignore the recent history of student protest. If accepted, the resulting plan might have, for instance, no separate departments and no administrative centre. If ignored, the plan would be conventional but it would be likely to provoke more protest later. In this case it might need extra buildings: for policemen.

Q. Is mystification inevitable if there is no theory, or
frame of reference, within which to take design decisions?

A. To me theories are safe but temporary stepping stones
across the dangerous waters of life, the unknown. But it is
the unknown, not theories or principles, that are the source
of the new. The whole point of transformation, the central
part of the design process, is to change what already exists,
and this includes both theories and practices. Each should
influence the other. To make theory the master of practice
is surely a form of repression! It is like being against one's
children, one's ideas, one's unrealised potential. To make
each responsive to the other is to create the conditions for
love not hatred.

(At one point the seminar was forcibly stopped while the
recording tape was changed. I objected to this as an example
of letting the machine control the man, the part the whole.
It seemed to me far better that some of the record was lost
than that everybody's train of thought be broken for an
ulterior technical purpose. This is an example of the very
high sensitivity of human action to technology and of the very
low sensitivity of technology to life.

How can this sensitivity be made to operate in two directions,
particularly when the technology concerned is large-scale, as
is a whole city?)

Q. Is there a conflict between designing, as a way of trans-
forming life, and dialectical politics, as a way of acting
historically against repression?

A. Within one's mind it is possible to see beyond both repress-
ors and repressed to utopian transformations of life in which
social conflicts are removed by the releasing of new life
patterns. But to apply utopian thinking, to make it real,
requires the political power to act against those who oppose
the utopia. A designer would ask if there is any non-destruct-
ive means of changing the consciousness of everyone. McLuhan

says there is. He believes that the existence of global
electric networks, such as TV, irresistibly change everybody's
consciousness by altering the mental processes by which we see
the world. "What if he's right?"[+]

Q. Surely it is necessary to have some goals during the
divergent stage of designing, when analysing the situation?

A. No. The purpose of divergence is to seek questions not
answers. The effect of divergence is to deliberately create
muddle and confusion in one's own mind, to upset one's own
assumptions so that one can become more sensitive to existing
reality and to new possibilities. There is no reason to fear
chaos: it is our name for another form of order: that which
we see as yet only in part. After exploring chaos one tries
to "surface", to recover one's mental balance, to create a
new picture of the problem, a transformation of the familiar
and contradictory world in the light of the many different
worlds it could become. But no transformation is possible if
one keeps to fixed goals or aims. Very often it is mental
certainty that turns out to be the underlying difficulty,
the hidden control, the barrier to living.

Q. I liked today's discussion because there was conflict: we
need conflict!

A. I did not like this conflict because too many speakers
assumed that there are only two possibilities: logical agreement about theory or else a dialectic clash. Few seemed to
believe that the deliberate searching for new syntheses by
immersing and losing oneself in chaos is possible. But without this one is tied forever to the known and is incapable
of dealing with what is uncertain, what is as yet beyond
man. Historically we can see that "man" has always managed
to reach what lies beyond. Woman too.

Q. What real difference is this plan* for a new university

*At this point we began to discuss plans for re-siting the
the University of Bologna. +The title of Tom Wolfe's essay.

supposed to make to the lives of the people in it?

A. Apparently very little. To me it is hopeless even to discuss urban planning because it operates at too low a level to have any answer to this critical question. The new design methods are capable of being used at this higher level, that of life as it is lived, but nobody has yet tried to use them radically, in this way. What a challenge!

Q. What are the main constraints and variables in this planning situation? How stable or unstable is this view of what the constraints and variables are?

A. It seems, from the models and plans, that many things that will change during the life of the buildings (eg the existence of departments) have been built into the plan. In the accompanying book of the planners' thoughts and methods nobody has asked any fundamental questions about the activities of the people who will live in the new university. For instance how long will it be before education is carried out decentrally, using information media and practical experience of life, instead of centrally, using lecture rooms, libraries and laboratories?

Q. Why base a plan on traffic movements? Surely the activities which generate the traffic are more important.

A. Yes they are, but so far our new methods enable us to deal with traffic but not with the reasons for travelling. Is there a method of dealing with these too?

. . . .

References:

McLuhan, Marshall, Understanding Media, McGraw-Hill, New York, 1964.

Wolfe, Tom, 'What If He's Right?', in McLuhan Hot and Cool, edited by Stearn, Gerald Emmanuel, Dial Press, New York, 1967, (originally published as 'The New Life Out There', New York Herald Tribune, 1965).

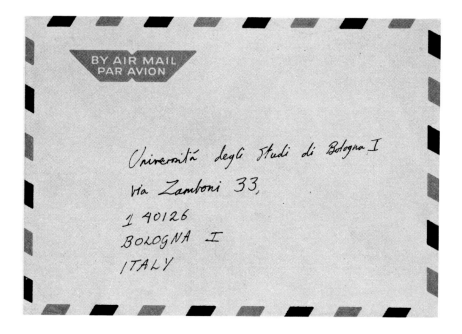

4th August 1982:

I remember thinking what a pity it was that the planners were
thinking of moving half of the University of Bologna out of the
historic city centre into a plate-glass building in the hills.

Surely everyone would prefer to remain in the old city if that
were possible?

Perhaps with new technology it is.

Why not build an exact replica of every detail of Bologna I
on a site nearby
with exactly the same university buildings,
and all other buildings,
in which another set of people could continue the same style
of life:
Bologna II?

how my thoughts about
design methods have changed
during the years

This was written for Day Ding, in 1974, when he asked me to
lecture to the architects at Illinois Institute of Technology
at Urbana. He suggested the topic. The text has been left in
the original American typescript because retyping on this
typewriter would have changed the original line lengths and
hence the intention.

A paper written for the EDRA conference is described in the
essay: it appears later in this volume under the title Is
Designing A Response To The Whole Of Life?

The essay appeared first as an open letter to Day Ding in my
book Dear Architects published as a limited edition at the
College of Architecture at Virginia Polytechnic Institute and
State University in 1974. It was published in Design Methods
and Theories, volume 11, 1977, pp. 50-62, in Spanner 17, Aloes
Books, London, 1979, and in Spanish in Summarios, volume V, 28,
Buenos Aires, 1979.

HOW MY THOUGHTS ABOUT DESIGN METHODS HAVE CHANGED
DURING THE YEARS

You don't know where you are
You don't know which way you're going

IN THE LATE FORTIES I BEGAN TRYING FOR WHAT I'D NOW
CALL A HUMAN FUNCTIONALISM ie MAKING DESIGN THOUGHTS
PUBLIC SO THAT THEY ARE NOT LIMITED TO THE EXPERIENCE
OF THE DESIGNER AND CAN INCORPORATE SCIENTIFIC KNOWLEDGE
OF HUMAN ABILITIES AND LIMITATIONS.

Surely that's one of the most human things in life
To be wrong
We all know that we have more affection for others when they're wrong
than when they're right
Sad, perhaps.
Some people called them systematic methods originally,
They've been mainly rational.

WHAT I BEGAN TO DO WAS TO RELATE DESIGN THINKING TO
OBJECTIVE OR SCIENTIFIC FACTS ABOUT HUMAN PERFORMANCE.
WHAT IS NOW CALLED ERGONOMICS.
OR HUMAN ENGINEERING.

ALSO I WAS TRYING TO ANTICIPATE NOT IGNORE SIDE-EFFECTS.

This still has not been done, or applied at any large scale outside

the military fields.

But to apply this knowledge to life in general seemed to me

And still seems

An appropriate thing to do.

But it couldn't be done unless the design process

The thinking

The reasons

That led to the lines on the drawing board

Could be spoken about in clear language

Such as a scientist uses when he writes a paper about how people do

this, or how metals do that.

But the design process was illogical and all this knowledge was logical

So until you had a logical design process

You couldn't join the two together.

Could the car be adapted much more to the people inside it?

We looked in enormous detail at the process of eating

We discovered all the kinds of food and all the actions of eating

The result was nothing like the knives and forks we now use

Our designs looked much more like dental instruments

IN THE FIFTIES I WORKED IN THE ELECTRICAL INDUSTRY TRYING

TO FIT DIALS, CONTROLS, SEATS, CONTROL ROOMS ETC TO THE

HUMAN OPERATORS.

THERE WAS ALSO THE GROWING NEED TO DESIGN LARGER ENTITIES

THAN PRODUCTS: COMPLETE SYSTEMS OF MACHINES, GROUPS OF

BUILDINGS, URBAN CENTERS.

Everyone was coming to realize that all was not well with technology after

all, it was creating problems as well as solving them.

All the equipment I'd ever handled seemed very badly designed in that

none of it took account of side effects,

Road accidents for example.

I suppose the trip to the moon is the best example of a complete system

which eventually worked after many failures and which used this kind

of thinking

IN THE SIXTIES THE SITUATION CHANGED

THERE WERE MANY CONFERENCES ON DESIGN METHODS

ENVIRONMENTAL SYSTEMS AND RELATED TOPICS.

I WROTE THE BOOK DESIGN METHODS,* A REVIEW OF THE

LITERATURE, AND I BECAME A TEACHER OF DESIGN

AND I BECAME ACTIVE IN WHAT'S NOW CALLED FUTURES RESEARCH

They all wanted a complete recipe,

It appeals to the Latin mind, especially,

A lot of the design methods literature has been translated into Spanish

and Italian, I'm sure its no accident that this is so.

There was one student who came to us from Argentia

"When" he said

"Chris, are we going to get the Grand Panoram?"

And this grand panoram didn't exist as far as I knew,

But he expected a complete ideology

Worked out & fully finished.

Many people wanted this and perhaps all students want it all the time

But I feel one should resist any such thing

If one's to continue living

Other than in the form of a

Intellectually speaking

Or actually speaking

I WAS SEEKING TO RELATE ALL THE DESIGN METHODS TO EACH

OTHER,

AND TO EXPERIENCE.

I FOUND A GREAT SPLIT HAD DEVELOPED BETWEEN INTUITION

AND RATIONALITY, REASON.

THERE WERE BLACK BOX METHODS LIKE SYNECTICS WHICH WORKED

WELL BUT NOBODY KNEW WHY

AND GLASS BOX METHODS, LIKE DECISION THEORY, WHICH WERE

LOGICALLY CLEAR BUT WHICH DIDN'T WORK.

What I could see was this...

What did I find out...?

We'll I found,...

In writing it...,...that book

A standard method of describing each method, so that they could be

compared.

What's striking is that each method begins with a first stage that is

extremely difficult to do

Which has no description of how to do it

Which is intuitive.

WHAT EMERGED

IN WRITING THE BOOK

WAS THAT TO USE DESIGN METHODS ONE NEEDS TO BE ABLE

TO IDENTIFY THE RIGHT VARIABLES

THE IMPORTANT ONES

AND TO ACCEPT INSTABILITY IN THE DESIGN PROBLEM ITSELF

ONE HAS TO TRANSFORM THE PROBLEM AND THE SOLUTION ALL IN ONE MENTAL ACT OR PROCESS

Where is the essence of the subject?

For me the word in the index with the most sub-entries to it

Is "Instability of Design Problems"

Which has about ten entries

The whole problem becomes more unstable as you widen it

As you take more and more of life to be part of the problem you

don't get a more stable problem you get a less stable problem.

And this I think is not what the rationalists like.

I think that people who approach this subject because it seems

rational are those who like certainty in life.

If you wish for certainty you might as well leave this subject alone

Because design is to do with uncertainty

As far as I can see

But a lot of people who do wish for certainty do dabble in it

And I fear they're wrecking the subject

. . . .

Especially transformation became evident...

How to get from divergent thought to convergent thought.

I WAS AT THE TIME DOING DESIGN RESEARCH INTO CAR SEAT
COMFORT, OFFICE DESKS, SLIDE RULES USABLE BY SCHOOL
CHILDREN, AND TRAFFIC AUTOMATION SYSTEMS

Incredible isn't it, the world is full of things, like slide rules, that
college students with an IQ of 120 or more, can use, and the rest of
the population, with a normal IQ, of 100, can't use.
Things like telephone handsets, which are used by the public, are
extremely difficult things to design
Because you've got to design them so that a very large percentage of
the whole population can use them.
A very interesting concept this
What percentage of the population can use your design.
You may say, if you're designing a building, that the whole lot can use it.
But I wonder.
The number of people who are too big or small to use it is quite high, millions.
Large numbers of old people, children and poor people don't use telephones
They've never got used to the difficulty.
They may use them for local calls but they can't possibly cope with
complicated calls.
Even though its an extremely easy thing to use and there are operators
waiting to help you.

IN THE SEVENTIES I REACTED AGAINST DESIGN METHODS.

I DISLIKE THE MACHINE LANGUAGE THE BEHAVIOURISM, THE CONTINUAL ATTEMPT TO FIX THE WHOLE OF LIFE INTO A LOGICAL FRAMEWORK.

ALSO THERE IS THE INFORMATION OVERLOAD WHICH SWAMPS THE USER OF DESIGN METHODS (IN THE ABSENCE OF COMPUTER AIDS THAT REALLY DO AID DESIGNING).

I REALIZE NOW THAT RATIONAL AND SCIENTIFIC KNOWLEDGE IS ESSENTIAL FOR DISCOVERING THE BODILY LIMITS AND ABILITIES WE ALL SHARE BUT THAT MENTAL PROCESS, THE MIND, IS DESTROYED IF IT IS ENCASED IN A FIXED FRAME OF REFERENCE.

My experience of design methods in the seventies has been of writing papers against the subject.

I received a letter asking me to write a paper for the EDRA conference and instructing me how to do it.

The writer of the letter outlined in ten pages what were the conditions applying to writers of papers for this conference

Use no more than five pages.

He'd adopted the whole language of behaviorism   to describe to his captive authors exactly how they should do their papers.

And much as I like the man who wrote the letters, I like him very much really as a person, I still felt pretty annoyed at this sheaf of instructions he sent out

And I thought to myself "I wont give this paper, I'm damned if I'm going

to...after all this time in this field to be told by him...he probably wasn't

alive when I started in it...exactly how to write a paper."

And I felt how insulting really that we have all this mass of machine

language instruction which we send to each other

In a bureaucratic manner

Throughout life.

Not only for arranging conferences.

. . . .

At that time I suddenly got interested in chance processes

And I discovered the works of John Cage

All about how to use chance to compose music and to compose lectures

And he says in there

If you receive a nasty instruction

You could refuse it,

You could protest strongly to the person who sent you the instruction

Or you could do what he John Cage does which is, apparently,

To obey the instruction & then do more.

Its tedious & arduous but a nicer way of responding

So I braced myself a bit

I stomached all the instructions

In five pages exactly.

24

I composed the paper by chance

Its got characters in it who speak

Its got a character called EDRA

And its got Walt Whitman, who speaks another kind of American other than

machine language

Its got Kant, who speaks machine language very much better than we designers

do

Its got Jung who says that no method is any good unless the right person

uses it

(which is an ancient Chinese view taken from The Secret of the Golden Flower)

And its also got some remarks by Graham Stevens

The man who left architecture as a student in the sixties to become one of

the leading people in inflatables, or blow-ups.

Perhaps you saw him walking on water at the EDRA conference

In a blown up plastic bag.

I introduced Graham into the paper because his account of how he did it

was so clear-cut.

He said

"We were fooling around with balloons & one day we got the idea of making

them huge & filling them with water, all sorts of things, and that led to

my life in inflatables."

Behaviorism, of the Skinner kind, had taken total command of the

architectural part of design methods by this

and I still feel that's a mistake.

WHAT I'M DOING NOW IS EXPERIMENTING WITH CHANCE PROCESSES

(THIS PAPER IS COMPOSED OF A CHANCE MIX OF MY LECTURE

NOTES, IN CAPITALS, AND RANDOM SAMPLES FROM A TAPE

RECORDING OF THE LECTURE, in small letters).

I AM ALSO TRYING TO FIND WAYS OF INCREASING PERCEPTION,

AND OF REDUCING ACTION, IN DESIGN, SO THAT WHAT'S NEW

IS MORE SENSITIVE TO WHAT'S ALREADY THERE.

I'M REALISING THAT IF DESIGNING IS APPLIED TO LIFE, NOT

JUST TO PRODUCTS, SYSTEMS AND SOFTWARE, THERE HAS TO

BE MORE POLITICS (IN THE ATHENIAN SENSE) (TWO-WAY PROCESSES)

AND LESS PLANNING,

IF DESIGNING IS NOT TO BECOME TYRRANY.

I'D LIKE TO TRY OUT EXPERIMENTAL DESIGNS, WITH NO CLIENTS,

AIMED AT RESPONDING TO LIFE AS A WHOLE NOT JUST TO A

SECTION OF IT

AND,

TO COMPENSATE FOR THE EXCLUSIVELY VISUAL & SPATIAL

QUALITY OF DESIGNING AS IT WAS

I'M TRYING TO LEARN FROM THE TEMPORAL ARTS: POETRY,

FILM, MUSIC & THEATRE.

SOME CONCLUSIONS

What seems to have happened is this:

– an extension of the scale and influence of design processes, to take
account of side-effects and of the integration of products into systems

– a search for greater precision & certainty in knowing what fits human
bodies and abilities

– greater uncertainty and instability of design problems as they include
more of life.

– psychological & social resistance to these effects, resulting in design
methods being neglected by the professional designers but florishing
as a rational but useless academic game.

– political resistance to the extension of planning, to the fixing of life
in a rational mould

– data overload (as yet unhelped by computer aids) which prevents designers
applying the vast existing knowledge which could otherwise permit a
truly "human functionalism"

Generally design seems to be becoming a social art & to do this properly
it seems we need to learn from experimental artists whose happenings &
other events are making art a way of living.

Both art & design at last seem like meeting, across the Cartesian
split of mind from body, to enable us to find a new genius for collaboration

not in the making of products & systems & bureaucracies but in the

composing of contexts that include everyone, designers too.

To be a part.

To find how to make all we do & think relate to all we sense & know,

(not merely to attend to fragments of ourselves & our situations.)

It was a question of where to put your feet.

It became a matter of choosing the dance

Now its becoming

No full stop

*Design Methods, John Wiley & Sons, New York & London, 1970.

now we are numerous

introduction to the Spanish edition of
Design Methods

The Spanish edition of Design Methods was published as Metodos de Diseno, translated by Maria Luisa Lopez Sarda, by Editorial Gustavo Gili, S.A., Barcelona, 1977. The third amplified edition, with additional material translated by Esteve Riambau i Sauri and bibliographic revision by Joaquim Romaguera Ramio, was published by Editorial Gustavo Gili S.A., Barcelona, 1982. Permission to reproduce this essay is gratefully acknowledged.

The reference to 'being numerous' on the last page was inspired by the verse:

> Obsessed, bewildered

> By the shipwreck
> Of the singular

> We have chosen the meaning
> Of being numerous.

from the long poem Of Being Numerous by George Oppen which appears in the book of that title published by New Directions Books, New York, 1968.

I have been asked to write an introduction to the Spanish edition
of Design Methods so that readers in Spain, Portugal and Latin
American countries will know what I now think of the subject
and of its application to the problems of the present time.

My thoughts about the subject have not changed since, in the
late forties, I found myself drawn to find ways in which it
might be possible to make the man-made world of machines and
industrial living better fitted to human life. At that time I
imagined myself to be alone in this search because all the machines
and ways of living with machines that I knew of seemed in some
profound indefinable yet very real way to be inhuman; yet they
are the main results of human effort through many centuries.
Today, after a quarter century, an amazing quarter century, of
efforts to humanize industrial life and methods, the problem
remains unsolved; but its now much bigger.

During these years I found I was not alone in wanting to find
ways of removing the obvious inhumanity from industrial work and
planning; there have been many designers, thinkers, critics and
activists who have tried in a variety of ways to change the
methods and practices of the professions and to bring the public
into the processes by which industrial life is formed. Some of
these methods I described in the original introduction to this
book and others have appeared since. But something has gone
wrong. In ways that are clearer to me now than when I wrote it
this wealth of new thinking seems not to have had the effects
expected, at least by myself. Instead of being the means by
which professional practices in design and other fields could be
despecialized and made more sensitive to human needs the new
methods have become convenient tools for larger and more rigid
planning and have also become the means of making design into
a barren academic subject removed from life, from the lives of
those for whose benefit its supposed to exist, ourselves as consumers and users of industrial products. More and more we recognise ourselves not as users of industrial life but as non-persons,
tools, objects that are used by the system. What has gone wrong?

It is tempting to blame the methods, to say that they are

inherently abstract, technocratic, inhuman, that they are a part
of the inhumanity which persons such as myself say we were trying
to remove from industrial products and the life that goes with
them. It is equally tempting to blame the professions, the system,. the status quo, to say that the new methods have never been
properly used but have been resisted, that they have been limited
to narrow applications which support specialization and prevent
the questioning of the way of life. Certainly I would now agree
that it was naive to have imagined that methods by themselves
(and they are not selves, they are, as I found myself writing in
chapter 5, "mere symbolic contrivances") that methods alone would
remove the error of centuries of industrial evolution. But to
imagine that it is possible to change the pattern of industrial
life without, among other things, a collective language to replace
and make public the up-to-now private and largly unvoiced thinking
of professional designers and planners is surely naive too. One
of the things I discovered while writing this review of the
literature on design methods was, as is explained in chapter 6,
that there is a big distinction between system-designing (which
fits products to each other and to existing social organizations)
and the wider process of what I then called socio-technical
change (the fitting of products and systems to newly emerging
forms of society). The section of this book that I most enjoyed
writing, but which I'm sorry to say is the least used so it seems,
was chapter 5, and particularly the last part of it in which the
purpose of design methods is discussed. Re-reading that today I
recall the sentence in which I attempted to condense this purpose
as I see it: "methodology should not be a fixed track to a fixed
destination but a conversation about everything that could be
made to happen."

So to me now, as in the past, the purpose of seeking changes in
methods not only in design but in all departments of life is to
change the pattern of life as we make it, artificially and
collectively, not to support the status quo and the inhumanities
we inherit but to permit the composing of a form of life that is
free of the errors of specialization and of alienation. To make
a way of living that is beautiful, (can laws be beautiful, can
work, can millions of people act together as trusted friends not

as distrusting manipulators of each other's lives?), to attempt
the best we can imagine and to use all intelligence to make it
real.

This aim, this purpose, this ideal, is not, I see now, implicit
in the methods, in the ink and paper in which they are composed.
Any aim that was would be a form of built-in control, another
inhumanity. The new methods can, like the alphabet and the
numerals, be used to say no or to say yes. But, like the alphabet, they permit communications that are otherwise impossible,
they increase the scale of human action and in doing this they
make ideals such as that I've just proposed more possible than
they were before. New methods cannot force us to do good, nothing
can, but they do change the context of designing. There is a
morality in widening the scope of life; what was before inevitable
becomes now a conscious choice. And once this widening, this
prior liberation, has occurred it is no longer realistic but
insulting to refuse the new ideals and purposes that now are possible. Industrial life HAS changed its nature in recent years
and thus includes the means of pursuing aims never tried before.
Of course the enlargement of what is possible includes the enlargement of what is bad as well as good, that is the risk,
unavoidable. A new responsibility for which the institutions
and professions and roles we inherit are surely unable by their
form and nature to respond.

Why then is there no sign of a new and larger beauty emerging
in the form of human life, why do we see nothing but growing
problems and greater inhumanities in the patterns of industrial
development throughout the world? And why, in design and planning,
are the new methods being used, if they're used at all, to make
life more uniform homogenous and alienating? The question feels
too difficult to answer but I'll try. Is it because we have
refused, so far, to see ourselves as real, as persons not as
ciphers, not as the objects which industrial living has forced
us to become? Is it that we have accepted as natural a bleak
vision of human nature, of man as the paid and helpless minder
of machines needing to do nothing but survive in ever growing
numbers? There are now several billion of us and soon more and

I for one rejoice in that. I cannot see that the presence of
people is a problem if it is allowed that each of us is really
human, whatever role it is the system has recently been forcing
us to play. We ARE numerous:that is the challenge, the new excitement of life now as it never was before. It's time to change
our aims, to see ourselves collectively as different, as able to
respond to the new conditions of human life.

In writing these words I recall with pleasure the many Spanish
speaking students, good friends, who have come to study design
methods here in Britain, and particularly Arturo Montagu of
Argentina who suggested that this introduction should be written.

J.C.J.
London, 1976

beyond rationalism

an interview

with questions by Marina Waisman,
Arturo Montagu and Ricardo Blanco

Marina Waisman edits the architectural journal Summarios and teaches architectural history at the Catholic University at Cordoba.

Arturo Montagu is a design consultant and teaches design research at the Universities of La Plata and Belgrano.

Ricardo Blanco is an industrial designer and teaches industrial design at the University of La Plata.

The interview took place at the Summarios office in Buenos Aires in April 1979. A version of it was published in Spanish in Summarios number 28 in 1980. It is reproduced here with permission of Ediciones Summa S A, Buenos Aires.

The typing of this version was a little experiment in trying to find a form of writing that retains some of the liveliness of speaking-while-thinking and does not impose on it the order of grammatical texts. In all but a few lines I have retained as much of the informative pausing, hesitating, and revising-while-saying that I could perceive in the transcript. I was surprised to see how much more intelligent speech appears when one reproduces its accidents than when one edits it into grammatical form.

Marina Waisman began the interview by referring to the article
How My Thoughts About Design Methods Have Changed During The
Years. She said how surprised she was, and glad, to see so
poem-like a piece of writing coming from one she had imagined
to be concerned only with the rational approach to design.....

CJ: There was a phase in the sixties
when many architects had a mania for design methods
but
it wasn't everyone that had the mania
I think it was only the rational part of design methods
which became popular
and it only became popular
with the kind of person who is very keen on rationality.
In this paper which you pointed to
I think I say something about certainty.
The rational method
gives you the impression you can solve the design problem
with certainty
with mathematical certainty
and the kind of person who likes that
is not really a designer.
He is a person who should never have been in design.
It is not to do with certainty, design.
Design is creating the new.
The new is always uncertain
that's the whole idea
and you do need rationality
but you need it to allow you to have the courage
the courage to expand further.
Rationality is usable to help you go along the way
into more uncertainty.
But the rationalist's decision theory
for instance
creates a box of a million possibilities
and then
like a machine
you look at these possibilities.
But its not the idea of looking at each item in the box

the list of all possibilities.
The real creative thing is finding where the edge of the box
    comes
and then saying
OK
what's outside it?
You couldn't look outside until you had the box.
It expands your view.
But to spend your life in the box is sort of wrong
as you...

MW: That's the idea of the blackbox
where you put everything that you can't understand

CJ: No. That's not quite right.
The black box is a more creative idea
the glass box is the rationality
where you can see everything

MW: But (whatever?) this blackbox is
you put inside everything you don't know where...

CJ: I don't think you're quite right there
the black box idea is your own brain
its not something outside the brain
and its called black box in cybernetics
because nobody knows how the brain works.
You know
something goes in through the eyes and ears
and something comes out from the mouth
and its a mystery.
So its called black box because its like the magician's box
you see
and that's the meaning of black box
so that one accepts the idea that there is a mystery
in the brain
and if there wasn't we couldn't be creative.

MW: But if you put the blackbox in a certain

and very definite
moment of the process,
its not true...

CJ: No, you do it all the time.
Yes, all the time.
These formal methods
for doing brainstorming or synectics
etc
I think they are valuable.
They are blackbox methods.
Its important to use them
I use quite a lot of formal methods
with some discipline
all the time.
But I try to use them in a new way each time.
The individual methods are not the whole design process.
The whole design process is everything you do
and other people do
and within this you may use this method
and that method
and something else you thought of
and a person comes into the room
and they say something
and that becomes part of what you do
and everything is the process.
And the really good thing
I think
about this subject of design methods
is that you should be more conscious
of how you organise your own design process
and not just be confused by it.
You should leave perhaps one third of your time
you know
for argument's sake
a good proportion of the time
to say
"Are we using the right process?"
Now

42

I would say its no delight doing this
because it stops you
you know.
I know it looks as if its going well
but then you say
"Are we going in the right direction?"
"How are we doing it?"
Keep on asking "How?"

MW: So you think that one must be conscious of the process...
at least at certain moments
not all the time?

CJ: Well, very often,
in designing a building
for instance
a house, or a hospital, or something,
its going...
and you know from the beginning
its going to be pretty like
the usual hospital
and the usual house
so, then,
its silly to use elaborate methods
and all this stopping.
But sometimes you're designing something nobody has ever done.
You're trying to design
for instance
a system of modular coordination
that's very difficult
and no-one has done one right yet
I think.
You know
I think all this modular work
so far
has been mainly wrong
and lots of modular systems exist
in architecture
but people don't like using them.

You have 'moveable partitions' and nobody moves them.
All this kind of thing.
They stay there like concrete
you know.
And there are all sorts of difficulties
like that of trying to make a building with new forms of energy
solar energy
and things.
Nobody knows how to do it.
So
you cannot use an existing process
when you're in that kind of problem
with novelty
and a need for innovation.
Then you need to 'design the designing'
let's say
as well as design the output of the designing.
And this designing the designing
is really the whole thing.
'Designing designing'
that gives the feeling of it
its a rather poetic phrase
rather than mechanical
it sort of lifts you up a bit?

MW: But what about all the new enthusiasm for typologies?

CJ: What is 'typologies', now?

MW: The idea of having a precedent type
a building type
and from this working on all the new projects.

CJ: I'm not familiar with this.
A new enthusiasm for typologies?
It sounds to me like what they used to do in the old days.

MW: Yes, this is the reactionary-vanguardist type...

CJ: I think we're now in a terrible period of looking back.
I think the sixties were
psychologically, politically, and sociologically,
and everything else,
upsetting for everybody.
And even the revolutionaries now
are wearing suits
and pretending that they like the 1930's
or some earlier period.
And everything you see on television,
people are dressing in pre-war clothes,
this kind of thing.

MW: Yes, yesterday I saw in a restaurant
a lady exactly like William Morris's wife.
It was incredible.

CJ: I call this the back-to period
you know
and I think of it like the waves of the sea.
I was brought up by the sea-side.
I used to watch the waves coming across
and they hit the promenade,
the stone wall,
and the wave made a big splash.
And then another wave is reflected back from the wall
into the sea
the reaction wave
and that destroys the next wave that comes.
And the second wave behind that
is also destroyed by the reaction wave
and it doesn't reach the wall either.
But this reaction wave then dies.
The reaction wave doesn't have much life in it.
Then another wave comes from the sea
and that does reach the wall!
I think that now in the seventies
we're in the reaction wave
and some pessimists think that the sea will produce no more waves.

But I think there'll always be waves from the sea
and that there will be no more reaction waves
unless the waves reach the wall.
Its only as a result of the success of the sixties
that we have the reaction.
There would be no reaction
if the sixties wasn't quite successful
I think.

MW: Well, that's a very positive way of looking.
I was thinking that the seventies were the day after the party
a beautiful party
and the day after that
we are disenchanted
and so sad
and with headaches
and all this...

CJ: No, I think positive things have a life of their own.
Negative things live on the life they borrow from the positive.
Negative things
in the whole of the universe
don't generate life.
So you need never fear the negative
because it is death
it dies very rapidly
its made of death.

MW: That was Croce's idea also
of history
that the negative periods
were only to make better...

CJ: Yes, but we do need the pause.
It could be very very useful
this pause.
The sixties were very confused
very muddled

very hopeless in many ways.
I didn't like the sixties much
because I was thinking of these things in the fifties myself
in the beat period of Kerouac
and all that.
That's when I felt
I first felt
some life.
And I thought a lot of the new things
which grew up in the fifties
new kinds of thinking
which became popular in the sixties
but when they became popular
they were really rather destroyed
by the form of the popularity.
They were misunderstood.

And I think in this pause period now
its an excellent time to say
"Well those sixties ways were not the right way to do it
they were too crude
they were frightening everybody
and they were not at all effective.
They had nothing positive about them
they were often very negative too..."
And take this rational thing we're talking about
you see
the worst aspect of design methods
the over-rationalism
was the one which became popular.
The good aspect
which is to combine rationality and intuition
which is much more difficult
than to JUST be creative, or JUST be rational
but to combine the two
that can't be done in the rush of a revolution.
Its a slow progress
and we can do that now
nobody's going to stop us.

Its a nice and quiet time.
We ought to think properly about what we are doing.

MW: But we are suffering from this reaction wave
and all these people
that in architecture at least
are figuring like vanguardists
and are a reaction...

CJ: Yes, but if you turn your attention from the producer
to the consumer
you lose this difficulty.
The consumers are more concerned with actual living.
The users of houses
etc
We're all users
you know
most of the time.
I know we're specialists
and avant guardists
and every other -ists
but first of all we have to have breakfast
and we sleep
and we're like everybody else
and we do that in buildings
as users of buildings.
And so if you think of that
you soon forget that the -isms ever existed
you know
because they're always superficial
even the good ones
you know
they're never the whole thing.
And I much prefer ordinary life
to specialism.
you know
sometimes I have a dream...
its so annoying that most of the people you meet
they dont know about any of the new things

so you can't talk about them with them.
Its irritating if you're keen on new things.
But then I go to a place where there are
where there are people who ONLY think of new things
and there's something missing
the ordinary life isn't there
what they call the real world's gone.
And then I walk down the street
I see all sorts of people who've never heard of any ideas
and its much more stimulating to me
in a way
because that is the real thing happening
you know
So if we go to the ordinary life
which we all live
even avant guardists are ordinary people
we look at our own ordinary life
that's the true inspiration
I think
and that's always there.

MW: That would have to do with the new interest in history
for all the buildings
and all the towns
and for conservation.
It would be a part of this recognising the life of the communiity

CJ: That's the good thing about this reaction we're in now.
What happens is that people in art and design
are no longer interested in formalism
they're no longer interested in shape
really
pure form
and abstraction.
They can no longer see any beauty in abstract expressionism
and all those things.
But all the beauty hasn't gone
its just that no one is looking for it any more.

And what they want to see
is how this affects the life.
And the new art forms are all social art
performance art
various forms of social art
concept arts
they're all non-visual
or else they combine two or three senses.
Its very interesting in painting now
there really isn't any painting
there's kinds of art which you can listen to
and you have to move around yourself to see it
or do it.
So they become dance-and-music-and-vision altogether.
I don't actually think that the arts which are limited to one sense
like painting to the eye
music to the ear
have any future any more.
Really what people seem to want
is arts that take more than one sense.
And so architecture is becoming not just visual
but social, thermal, temporal, historical.
I'm sure I don't know much about architecture really
but there must be something which you know
which will tell you
that more than one sense in the body
more than the eye
is coming in.
And after all its ridiculous
if you think about it
to have an art of one sense when everyone has got many.
And how did it ever arise?......
So no wonder people are baffled by painting
you don't normally look without hearing.
You normally integrate the senses.
Watching television
you see
is a **very** good example
of an art which uses two senses

and its much more popular than radio
which has one sense.

Ricardo Blanco: You always speak of two moments
the rational moment
the creative moment
the creative pause
two stages
the methodological one and the creative one.
Wasn't it possible to think about a division
between designers who think about problems
and designers who think about solutions?

CJ: Well, I don't like these divisions.
I was explaining yesterday
actually
Ricardo
in that lecture
that although
when you write about it
you have to write about rationality on one page
creativity on another page
problems on one page
solutions on another page
that's because writing is linear
because you have to think about them separately
but you don't do them separately
you do them integratedly.
You see in this book here
(I was looking at my own book, Design Methods, the Spanish edition)
I've found a certain chapter
chapter 5
the title of this chapter is in english
The Disintegration of Design Methods
I don't know how to translate it
The disintegration of the design process
(Looking now as I type I see that the title is
The Design Process Disintegrated)
now

I used the word disintegration there after a lot of thought
that was to warn the reader
that what you're getting in this chapter
which is the most integrated chapter in the book
I'm calling it disintegration
because
as I was saying in our analysis of the design process
with designing designing
if we are going to re-design designing
which we have to do
there's no choice about this
we have to at first understand the design process
and the process of understanding does benefit
from breaking things into pieces
but only realising that they fit together again.
There's a lovely quotation from Coleridge
who is often known as a poet
but in fact was a splendid philosopher
and Coleridge says
that there is a difference between the crude type of philosopher
or thinker
and the subtle thinker
the crude thinker takes things to pieces
and they remain in pieces
the subtle thinker doesn't make breaks in things
he makes distinctions.
Now
a distinction is recognising parts of something
which is a whole
and the example which Coleridge takes is the word 'thought'...

...there is a distinction between the two meanings
of the word 'thought'
and these are two distinct processes.
There is what happens to the thought
when you write it down
and communicate it to somebody
and there's the process by which you arrive at the thought...

...thought and thinking.
And in the same way
design and designing
problem and solution
are like this.
Everything really
night and day
all of these things.
Life is full of these opposites
apparent opposites
which very often are complements.
Complementarities.
And we are really wasting our time if we're not going to
    recognise
that what seems like opposites
are often complementaries.
Don't do anything unless you are prepared to recognise that.

(here I've omitted a long section describing details of
chapter 5, and other sections of the book, leading into a
description of a typical method)

And then another thing about reading the individual method
is that they all start with steps
one, two, three, four, five.
If you start with the first step
say on page 96
step one...
well, I can't read it in Spanish yet,
never mind...
step one is always very hard to do.
Its a non-rational step.
For nearly all the methods
however rational
step one is a non-rational step
and has to be done with
not only intuition
but with experience.
That is

intuition which is informed with experience.
Intuition which is not informed by experience
is a very misleading thing
very often.
Intuition which is based on the right experience
is the only really good guide we have in life.
And this is why you say
"that man's a fool, I don't believe him".
You know his intuitions are not based on experience
they just pour out of him
but you know he hasn't lived it.
Someone who speaks much less
sometimes
is perhaps...
you might even not think of him as creative
but they are
because the few words they use are informed by a lot of experience
and as well as imagination.
And that's the integration.
But you can't do this integrating in a book
you can only do it in yourself.

MW: ...so that's why I am more keen on the historic kind of
introduction to methodology
than the rational one.
In the historical analysis
if you keep only dividing,
analysing,
you never understand anything.
You destroy the works you're trying to understand.
It is always necessary to...

CJ: There are times
though
when you do not feel very intuitive.
You cannot make yourself be intuitive, imaginative,
you have to wait
and then
when that happens

you should stop
and do other things.
But even if you're feeling very tired
you can do some useful analysis.
THERE'S a distinction
Ricardo.
I think you can separate them in time a bit
you can do some analytic work
you don't need to be in a very inspired frame of mind
always
for it.

RB: Sorry, I didn't follow the last phrase.

CJ: Perhaps you could translate for Ricardo?

(here follows translation from English into Spanish)

(Marina Waisman then translates Ricardo's next question
into English:)

MW for RB: Very creative designers
when they approach the problem
they invent the problem.
They're so creative that they create the problem.

CJ: Well, I think Ricardo is quite right there.
You always have to invent the problem.
I don't think the prior existence of the problem is true.
I always hate the word 'human needs'.
I these guys who write 'human needs'
they imagine there's a dictionary up in the sky somewhere
where all the human needs
for all the future
are written down.
This is silly.
You're right that the needs exist
when the means of satisfying the needs exists.
There was no need for houses when people lived in caves.

And some man
some very inspired man
said "let's build a house"
and that was a great step.
And afterwards
when they got over the shock
some people preferred the house to the cave.
But there was no need for the house.
Life was perfectly allright in the caves.
Similarly with television.
There was no need for television.
And if you have colour television you can't do without colour
but before you had colour you'd see no reason for it.
Its three times as much money for hardly any improvement.
But when you're adapted to it...
so the need comes from being adapted.
That's all the need means
even the need to eat.
We know that people going in for fasting lose the need to eat
and they survive
for very long periods.
Even fundamental
seemingly fundamental things like that.
There are people in the world
who sleep for only quarter of an hour every night
and have lived this way for forty years
and they're perfectly ok
they've managed to live without sleeping.
And so you cannot find any fundamental human needs
that some freak hasn't done without.

Arturo Montagu: Le Corbusier,
when he speaks about the machine of living
is putting a concept which is extended to all the world
and is going to pressure also on the society
the modern society.
It is imortant to know the responsibility of the designer
how he interprets the situation.
When the designer develops the consumer's products

which is a different type of product
there is high motivation of the designer
to express himself through the product
which infact is his personal problem.

CJ: That's right.
You've completely got it.
That's his personal problem.

AM: Because we're always discussing in the faculty
this type of problem
because after a certain number of years
we come also to the problem of the students.
And its for us.
We are in both sides
the theoretical side and the practical side...
Its a key problem,
what he says.

(Ricardo Blanco speaks, in Spanish)

AM for RB: He says why the designer should feel guilty
about this expressiveness
about this need of expressing?

CJ: Well,
the functionalist aesthetic
of course
was an aesthetic of puritanism.
And it was a reaction against.
It arose in the Vienna Circle with Adolf Loos
and everything that comes from the Vienna Circle
the psychology that came from it
the philosophy that came from it
the music that came from it
the architectural theory that came from it
by all these great names

(I was thinking of Freud, Wittgenstein, Schoenberg, Loos)

they were all actually reacting against the wave
which couldn't or wouldn't go away
the wave of the Hapsburg Empire.
They were continuing imposed expressionism of the upper classes
on the buildings.
And they got rid of decoration and ornaments
as a cleansing.
They were all cleansers of a bad situation which had arisen.
and of course we no longer have to react against it.
That's over.
We don't like functionalism any more.
But that functionalism was never real functionalism
it was visual functionalism
it was formalism
masquerading as a function.
It wasn't really the function of the people in the building
or of the building.
It was the function of looking at it as if it was a function
and it was actually a visual style
and it was just as much self-expressive, in fact
as all the decoration of the older buildings.

I think what's nice now in architecture
are the very irrational buildings.
The ones I like are those which are amazingly functionless.
I, for instance, quite like the New York Five.
(line missing here)
they make it of wood and paint it to look like concrete
and
ok
it always was like that really.
They've been more truthful in fact
by admitting it was a decorative style.
And they take it to Palladian degrees
and,
you know,
make it more formal
and its only for rich men's houses
and it really hasn't much bearing on life

but there you are.
But the fact that fact that they are very spiritual is nice
and that's attractive.
We shouldn't remove spirituality in design
I think
in this whole business
because that's the inspiration of living.
But there are functional limits which really are negative
usefully negative.
They say there are certain forms of building
which are actually damaging to people.
And the functionalist theory
or the scientific analysis of building requirements
this tells you that if the pillars are thinner
and so on
the building will fall down and people will die.
That doesn't tell you how to do the building
it tells you how not to do the building
and that's negation.
The value of science is that its formalised negation
the method of science is not to prove things
but to work on the negative.
To disprove things.
That's why scientists are basically sceptical.
They work on
they're artists of the negative
we might say.
They use the negative to remove false ideas from the mind
and false assumptions.
We all make false assumptions
and only the scientists
at the end
have the courage really to test their assumptions
and they usually find they're wrong
they're happy to be wrong.
A scientist is a man who's happy to be wrong.
When he's wrong he discovers something.
And the rest of us haven't learnt this

particularly in design.
We have to manufacture a kind of certainty
in order to proceed
and a confidence
and so we are very unscientific.

But the really useful function theory
I think
doesn't come from avant guarde movements
it comes from the kind of design called ergonomics
which investigates the human being.
Ergonomics won't tell you what makes people happy
what makes people feel sublime.
But it can tell you what will give people headaches
and eyestrain
and backaches
and all those things.
But these are to do with the body.
The mind
ergonomics is a very bad guide for.
The kind of ergonomics that has got into design theory
is this wretched behaviourism
Skinner, and pidgeons, and all this stuff,
and this kind of behaviourism
is trying to apply physiological thinking to the mind
where its out of place.
And its great for the body.
So behaviourism is fine if you want to discover how people act
in a bodily way.
But these behaviourist models
afterwards made into a computer program now
to model the behaviour of people in a city or an urban area
I think are very dangerous
because they try to model what people's wishes and desires are
and what's on their mind
and this has to remain open.
If you plan this
then life is gone.
And they should limit themselves

these computer men and behaviourists
to the bodily thing.
But they don't have the modesty to do that...

(a confusing section of the transcript is omitted here)

MW: Really that's what you said
about the need for an intuition based on experience
and knowledge.
So there's a need for very much knowledge beforehand
and then you can free yourself...

(another confusing section)

CJ: Yes, that of course.
You see, there's a difficulty there
I think
and its this:
that when the building, the motor car, or whatever it is
is going to be fairly similar to the last one
and they nearly all are, actually...
...where that's the case
then you can get experience from the older ones
which are relevant.
But the typical modern problem is one like I said
with solar energy or something like that
which is quite a new concept
which there's no experience of.
Now
with that
you cannot find anybody who has the informed intuition.
Therefore you have to generate artificial experience.
I always say that the scientific part of the new design methods
is designing designing
is designing a quick education for yourself
as a designer.
The designer has to design an educational programme for himself
every time he designs
so that he learns rapidly enough to become experienced

and he makes his final decisions when he knows
that he is using experienced intuition.
He makes his initial guesses
which should be very wild
knowing that he is going to throw them away.
And the traditional designing method
in all fields
doesn't really allow for this.
Traditional design method
in architecture engineering and other fields
really starts with the chief architect or the chief engineer
in only a week or so
making all the major decisions
and this is very destructive
practically hopeless for what we are talking about.
Those decisions have to be taken in the last week of the process
not the first
and all the rest of the time should be spent with many people
not just the chief designer
or team
trying to educate themselves very quickly
and trying to lose their...
you see
experience you bring to a new problem
is experience of all the problems
is very misleading
you're happy with it
you're confident in it..
but it doesn't relate to this problem.
So you have to go through the process of unlearning.
And the most useful effect of the irrational methods in this book
is that they're very rigid
and I like that rigidity
because that rigidity forces you to unlearn.
You won't unlearn without a stick
you know
or a carrot or something
you know.
You need formalism to help you unlearn.

AM: All the need for alternative technologies
or alternative architecture
comes from a very good understanding of the bad ways
that architecture and technology have leaned to
so this kind of negative experience is necessary.
If not
you wouldn't think about the wind
or the water
or the sun.
So its the suffering of modern technology
the modern architecture...

CJ: Its very interesting
you see
that the curtain wall was a creative idea once.
It sounds quite a poetic word
'curtain wall'.
A curtain wall
you know
what a beautiful concept.
And now the curtain wall is the symbol
of all that's dreadful
in homogenous plastic architecture.
But what I was really thinking about the curtain wall
is this:
there's almost no curtain wall that doesn't leak
there's almost no curtain wall that doesn't have wind problems
and actually
though thousands of them have been made
there's very few cases where they've really solved problems
which in the brick wall
and the ordinary window
were solved centuries ago
because although we thought we knew how to solve them
we still can't really do it with the new materials.
Amazingly difficult.
Such a simple thing.

MW: Now you put in the air conditioners

but you don't think about the sun
and the glare
the terrible glare
and its very usual in Argentina
sometimes in my town
in Cordoba
which is very hot
and very sunny
its terribly brilliant
the sun
and you put a wonderful curtain wall
and then you can't live inside
it's impossible
you must wear sun-glasses inside.

AM: If not
you cannot work.

MW: You feel invaded
by all this glare...

CJ: Well, of course
this really comes from a religious point.
All the people in the 1930's were sun worshippers
they were disguised religiouses
they all claimed to be very irreligious
but they all worshipped sunlight.
The tower block was the idea that one should get sunlight
and the curtain wall was nature coming into the house.
What nobody said was "why do you have a house?".
Now
you have a house because
for most of the human things
which animals don't do
like reading
and writing in particular...
Have you ever tried to read and write on the beach?
It's terrible.
I mean the glare is impossible.

You cannot read anything
and the slightest bit of wind blows the papers around.
Those two simple things.
There's nothing flat enough to put things on
they roll off
and they get sand in them.
You just can't do what we're doing now on the beach
you know.
We'd have given up a long time ago
and gone for a swim perhaps.
It would have been better!
But
if you want to do these modern things
you have to have non-natural surroundings.
Whether we're wise in this I don't know.
We may be very unwise in the long run.

MW: I think man is now a cultural animal
lives in a cultural surrounding
and needs this cultural surrounding to...

CJ: Mind you
the new concept in design is sufficiently broad
to ask even big questions like
"Should we carry on writing?"
"And reading?"
"And locking ourselves up in boxes?"
"With or without our windows?"
you know.
And previously there was no way
in the architectural profession
or the engineering profession
for handling a question as big as that.
Now
I like to think that these new methods
which some people call a fringe movement in design
and I always say that this fringe movement is a bad name
given to new things by the old
the old people say its a fringe

its not a fringe
its the new centre!
The new thing makes the old into a fringe.

(some confused words here in the transcript)

...and this central new idea
of widening the design process
means that you don't use the process for the same things as
you use the old process for
you don't actually use these new methods for designing buildings.
There's very little in that book about designing buildings
its mainly about designing intangible things...

(a section about the appropriateness of formal design methods
to the designing of computer systems and software)

...design an educational system
a traffic system.
A traffic system has hardware in it
it has streets and buildings and cars and things
but the essence of it is the movement
which is somewhat intangible.
You're designing movement.

MW: So, the aims of design are conditioning the process of design.

CJ: The new process has new aims
it doesn't have the same aims
so its no good saying it has failed
as a means of designing buildings.
It wasn't meant for that.
It was meant to do what buildings won't do.
Buildings won't design the movement.

MW: But
for some time
we will still live and work in buildings.

CJ: We will always perhaps have buildings
but preferably buildings which are compatible
with a much more beautiful form of movement in life.
The movement we have in the city generally is ugly
it really is ugly
and it has never been considered as a subject for design
but now its very interesting that in the fine arts
they've been onto that for some time now.
They are trying to find ways
if you like
of making the movement of life beautiful.
That's what performance art is
that's what concept art is
its beauty of thought
or beauty of doing things.
They're starting off in rather seemingly ugly ways
because they're iconoclasts
but nevertheless what they're trying to do
in this least understood form of art
which is now appearing
is to look at life itself
at the movement if you like...

MW: Its very difficult
I think
to understand and to transmit
that you're designing non-tangible things.

CJ: Yes.
People say to me
you know
O, he has never designed anything.
I feel annoyed
because actually I've designed a traffic system
and a lot of intangibles.

MW: A traffic system is at least something that you can understand.

CJ: And designing the design process

is the most subtle of things...

(a section on the obstacles to a general recognition that it
is right to pay attention to the design of intangibles)

AM: I would like to make some remarks
about what Chris Jones feels
when I took him
not around Buenos Aires
but in our daily trip to La Plata.
What he was saying
is that when we were just moving through the Avienda Calchaquí
which for an architectural eye
or for our architectural feeling
is such a kind of chaos
with all the houses without any plan
all the houses different heights
the colours the form the morphology
he told me something which struck me.
He told me that "I am learning a lot about this country
when through this avenue
because I am seeing how the people feel
how the people live
how the people are doing things without professionals".
Then
and he was very happy that I was taking
this type of route
I said "Its the only route to La Plata"
although I was very frightened I must admit...
He was very frightened by the traffic (very fast & irregular)
and then he told me
please, if you can go slowly with the car
just because he wanted to look
not only because he was frightened.
He likes to look at these particular architectural things.
But then
when we entered the new route to La Plata
which they call Camino Centenario
which for us is a big improvement

this new way
with lighting at night and four ways
he said "Its not Argentina for me
because I saw the same route in Japan, America,
I prefer the Avienda Calchiqui".
This was my remark
according that all the movement of Chris Jones now is
he's against the
what he called the "world of plastic"
which is surrounding Europe and part of the United States
and his recommendation to us is
that we
as professors and designers
should try to avoid this type of situation
not to convert Argentina into a world of plastic.

CJ: I like the word 'homogenized'
because it identifies what's going wrong.
We produce the homogenized world
homogenized architecture
homogenized milk
and really we don't seem able to stop this.
I spent a year in Virginia Tech.
and there was a large department of architecture
which was itself in a rather homogenized building...
...they had many students
and they were all producing these little models.
I was curious about the models.
They were very elaborate
balsa wood
other kinds of material
plastic models really of the new buildings
and their forms were extemely irregular.
By now irregularity of form has become
in that architecture school
a new formalism.
It wasn't straight simple shapes
everybody had the most interesting complicated ground plan
and everything was curved

there was really nothing at right angles to anything any more
and you might think that that wasn't homogenized
and that the buildings which would come out of it
would not be.
But nevertheless
when you saw the models in a row
when you see the designs which have come out of them
it still has exactly the same feeling in the mind
of "we're in a homogenized world".
I'm sure that the architectural profession know this
and is very puzzled by their own situation
and can't see their way out.
I can't either.
Its a really baffling thing
but geometrical variety doesn't seem to get you out of it.

MW: No,
because you choose geometrical variety
instead of geometrical rationality
but its the same thing.

CJ: I think the surrealistic buildings
which are beginning to appear in the USA
I don't know if they are appearing here
with, for instance
a part of the wall broken away deliberately
and bricks tumbling down
you know the ones I mean
I can't remember the names of these architects...

MW: Yes, SITE. S.I.T.E., its one of the groups doing this.

CJ: That's right
with this sort of Salvador Dali approach
almost
to architecture.
That breaks out of it (homogeneity)
in a very strange way
because that is rather arresting

70

you know
it takes your attention
and very strongly
perhaps too strongly.
But I like that too because it is at least a beginning
of getting away from that kind of homogeneity.

MW: Yes, I think that this kind of vernacular architecture
and the respect for the local...can give some way of...

CJ: That book Architecture Without Architects
is very interesting visually.
Its a pity that the words in it don't somehow explain more.
Because nobody's understood more I suppose
and you can't ask the people
because they're not that kind of person.

AM: It could be very interesting to show Chris
something of our vernacular architecture...
Of which I suppose you are a specialist...

MW: We have some slides but I don't have them here.

CJ: When I go to Rosario is there something I can see?

MW: Rosario is a very new town
its a nineteenth century town.
Our town is a more colonial town.

CJ: Really I should go up in the hills
should I?
A long distance......

principles in design

Sydney Gregory, the editor of Design Studies, invited several
people to react to ten principles proposed by W. H. Mayall in his
book Principles in Design, published by the Design Council,
London, 1979. This review of the principles first appeared in
Design Studies Volume 1, number 3, January 1980, pages 182-3,
published by Butterworth Scientific Limited, PO Box 63, Westbury
House, Bury Street, Guildford, Surrey, GU2 5BH. I am grateful
for permission to reproduce it here together with quotations from
W. H. Mayall's book (with the permission of The Design Council).

Here are my reactions to the ten principles of design
formulated by W.H.Mayall. These are my first thoughts on
reading the principles alone.....without reference to what
Mr Mayall has to say about them in his book.

1. THE PRINCIPLE OF TOTALITY
    All design requirements are always interrelated and must
    always be treated as such throughout a design task.

Yes and no. The degree to which any pair of requirements
are related, which can vary from negligibly to critically,
depends upon which of many possible designs is chosen, eg
if one decides to provide a digital watch then the
requirements 'indicate the hour' and'indicate the date' are
likely to be strongly interconnected : not so if one
decides to provide a dial watch and a calendar.

2. THE PRINCIPLE OF TIME
    The features and characteristics of all products change
    as time passes.

Yes, but again one has to know the degree to which these change
before one knows whether it is going to affect one's design
decisions. A more useful principle would be one which helped
one to discover this, eg to ask the question 'to what extent
do the assumptions and decisions made in the proposed design
remain true for the expected life of the product?'.

3. THE PRINCIPLE OF VALUE
    The characteristics of all products have different rel-
    ative values depending upon the different circumstances
    and times in which they may be used.

Yes. The values differ also, I believe, according to which
of the possible alternative designs one decides upon, our
wishes being much conditioned by the availibility, or not,
of any means of satisfying them, eg the value of tv was to
most of us nil until we got used to it, equally the value of
colour tv was nowhere near 'three times the price' until we
got used to that.

4. THE PRINCIPLE OF RESOURCES
   The design, manufacture and life of all products and systems
   depend upon the materials, tools and skills upon which we
   can call.

But the materials, manufacturing processes, and the skills of
making, and of using, are all highly variable, and, I believe,
almost unpredictable. So,if we begin our design trying to
fit only the existing resources,we will miss most of the
opportunity for making something new and be led into
a too conservative result?

5. THE PRINCIPLE OF SYNTHESIS
   All features of a product must combine to satisfy all the
   characteristics we expect it to posess with an acceptable
   relative importance for as long as we wish, bearing in
   mind the resources available to make and use it.

This sounds like the writer straining to make a single
sentence embody a mass of conflicting requirements while
providing a single criterion to indicate success. To attempt
this is, I believe, to push language further than it will go.
I dont think there is a rational way to indicate that a design,
or any other composition, is 'right'. Measurement, and reason,
can each go part of the way, but, when it comes to assessing
the whole, each person is obliged, implicitly, to express his
or her view of life, his or her self, and these are
beyond what can be stated rationally. To attempt certainty,
with respect to the whole, is, I think, to take away the
opportunity to be oneself, or to act unpredictably, as a
person, not as a thing. I feel sure that one of the reasons
why the designed world has recently become to be experienced
as inhuman and over-homogenized is that we have tried to
seek this kind of rational certainty where only what used to
be called 'the heart' can speak. The place for science and
reason, in design, is a large one, but it is not in usurping
the imagination. It is in extending its range and sensitivity.

6. THE PRINCIPLE OF ITERATION

Design requires processes of evaluation that begin with
the first intentions to explore the need for a product
or system. These processes continue throughout all sub-
sequent design and development stages to the user himself,
whose reactions will often cause the iterative process to
continue with a new product or system.

Iterating, which I prefer to call repeating, or 'going back
to square one', is of course a common experience for designers.
It is to avoid the cost and delay of this that we have tried,
in recent years, to find more certain design methods (as well
as for the more positive aim of making things better in themselves, more usable, beautiful, and less harmful to bystanders,
more fitting to life as a whole). I believe that to be driven
back to square one is a confession of failure, something to
do as seldom as possible, an indication that one's design methods
are inadequate to the situation. Adequate methods will, I
believe, enable one to learn, in a pre-design phase, much of
what one may repeatedly fail to learn if one plunges ahead
without them. The right way to design a design process is to
recognise that one is trying to give oneself the experiences,
early in designing, which will teach all those unexpected things
that one often learns about the product, and its context, only
when it is too late.

7. THE PRINCPLE OF CHANGE

Design is a process of change, an activity undertaken not
only to meet changing circumstances, but also to bring
about changes to those circumstances by the nature of the
product it creates.

I like this principle, it is one which has been absent from
much of what has been thought and written about design: the
realizing that the problem and the solution are interdependant.
New possibilities change our picture of the world and change
our ideas of what we need. It is for this reason that I am
critical of the attempt, in some of Mr Mayall's other principles

as well as in much recent design methodology, to stabilise
requirements by ascribing to them values on a rational or
numerical scale. To allow, in designing, for the interrelation
of requirements and possibilities is to admit to life, to
what makes things worth doing for their own sake, to all that
is beyond the reach of calculation. Without this, design
is a form of social control, a perpetuation of ourselves as
we were, not an exploration of how we may become.

8. THE PRINCIPLE OF RELATIONSHIPS
   Design work cannot be undertaken effectively without
   establishing working relationships with all those activities
   concerned with the conception, manufacture and marketing
   of products and, importantly, with the prospective user,
   together with all the services he may call upon to assist
   his judgement and protect his interests.

I like this principle too, but I don't think it goes far
enough. What I understand it to mean is that designing is
no longer a solo activity but, increasingly, the concern of
many experts, users, pressure groups, and others, all of
whom are more·strongly affected by the results of designing
now that what we make is more powerful, of a larger scale,
and more highly interconnected, than it was. What this
calls for is, I think, more than 'establishing working
relationships with all those activities concerned'. It
requires collaboration, on an increasingly equal basis, and
a sharing of the responsibilities, which designers, so far,
keep to themselves. 'But only a single mind can create'
we might say to ourselves, 'not everyone, and certainly no
committee, can exercise design skill'. Yes and no. The kinds
of design skill which are presently taught and practiced by
the design professions are adapted to the assumption that
one mind is adequate to designing in the new situation of
increasing interconnectedness in which we find ourselves, but
it is not adequate. And the kinds of design skill which
are called for in using the newer design methods, which the
professions as yet do not seem to take seriously, are suited

to collaboration, to the sharing of responsibilities between
users and experts, and to designing imaginatively in a
collective process, as was the case in craft evolution.

9. THE PRINCIPLE OF COMPETENCE
    Design competence is the ability to create a synthesis
    of features that achieves all desired characteristics
    in terms of their required life and relative value,
    using available or specified materials, tools and skills,
    and to transmit effective information about this synthesis
    to those who will turn it into products or systems.

Here again is something that I am beginning to recognise
throughout these principles : the attempt to pack, into
single sentences, the increasingly wide-ranging criteria by
which the increasingly over-loaded centre, the designer,
is to measure his success in meeting increasingly wide-
ranging requirements that his work has to satisfy. At what
point do we recognise that centralized designing ceases to
be effective and becomes an obstacle, and not the means, to
'good design'. Surely there is such a point. I believe we
have already passed beyond it and that it is time to rethink
designing, design education, and the need for design professions,
in relation to the growing dissatisfaction with technology,
design, planning, and their effects. The new competence which
the situation now requires is, I believe, not that of deciding
the shape of a product or system but the shape of a new
context or process in which everyone, not just designers or
experts, is enabled to see what is needed of him or her if
the form of industrial life is to get better, for everyone,
and not worse. To arrive at this is not to continue to design
but to do something at a different scale from that, the scale
of the whole problem, the scale of decentral action, thought,
imagination.

10. THE PRINCIPLE OF SERVICE

Design must satisfy everybody, and not just those for
whom its products are directly intended.

I dont think that this is any longer an ideal, a voluntary
extra, something to be done only when one can afford it. It
has already become a necessity that new products are assessed,
discussed, researched, and tried out in unharmful ways, before
they are launched to ensure that they do not cause more harm
than good. But the present way of attempting this, through
centrally organised design, market research, technology
assessment, drug testing, planning, operations research,
etc, has not only got beyond what a single design profession
can do, it is failing to correct the increasingly obvious
fault of industrial life : that it is becoming impersonal,
homogenized, an inhuman system that does not seem, in the
way it has been set up, to recognise us all as persons. What's
to be done? Far more, I think, than to present overloaded
professionals with exhortations to act by better principles.
To do that is, I'm sorry to say, to make things worse, for
it diverts energy and good will to a scale of action
that cannot work when it could be applied to one that will.
The best service, the bravest, is to stop designing, in the
ways we do now, and to try for something better. To raise
our individual thoughts to the scale of our collective actions.
And to give ourselves the space to act accordingly.

largon It they itsnowifatjohns geth
rubcit path

for onedofybleachedthey night?

John Cage
Empty Words

2
THE WORLD WITHOUT IMAGINATION

St Ives by chance

I was invited to contribute to the lecture series 'Description: Invention: Reality' organised by Ranulph Glanville and Annetta Pedretti at the Architectural Association, London, in 1979-80. The lectures appeared in a special issue of aaq, the Architectural Association Quarterly, volume 12 number 4, 1980, edited by Dennis Sharp in consultation with Ranulph Glanville. The essay is reproduced with the permission of the Architectural Association Quarterly.

Ranulph told me that his lecture series had a connecting idea:
that things designed, and perceived, are influenced, perhaps
more than we think, by the perceptions, the ways of seeing, of
ourselves as designers and perceivers. Those are not his words:
they are the words that are close to my memory of what he said
and may well be quite far from those he used, memory being so
largely the inventing of details which support our present
feelings about some past event which we have forgotten in its
details and which we may not have paid much attention to at the
time. (That, as I understand it, is the gist of the analysis
of memory in Frederick Bartlett's book Remembering, published
in the early thirties and still, perhaps, one of the truest
writings about memory?)

Looking in my slide collection for something in the spirit of
this idea I chose some slides made in 1972 when I was on a
family holiday in St. Ives. I was tired of the beach, and of
being limited to the things that a holidaymaker is expected to
do. And I'd been reading one of John Cage's books (A Year From
Monday) and beginning my attachment to his ideas, which has
lasted ever since. I noticed that, in one of his writings, he
says that the invention of the camera, the Kodak box camera
that anyone can use, was just the kind of step he likes: a
move that shifts the 'artistic' role, and 'skill', from the
specialist to the amateur, the ordinary person. I wondered
how John Cage would himself use a camera, and, as I knew of no
example of him doing so, I decided to guess what he might do
with it. I asked my daughter Sarah to lend me her Instamatic
for the afternoon and set out to try to photograph St. Ives in
the manner of John Cage, as near as I could manage, knowing him
only through his books.

I looked first at the picture post-cards of St. Ives and
immediately realised now very close to these views, carefully
chosen for being 'typical' or 'picturesque', are ALL the
holiday photos we take, by the million. (How odd that certain

views of the earth, and of ourselves, are photographed so
repeatedly, each summer, with such pleasure yet with so little
'originality'.) I decided that what John Cage would do, with
an Instamatic, was to remove intentionality from the choosing
of the views to be photographed. Instead, I guessed, he'd
leave the decisions as to where and when to point the camera
to chance. Not just to a careless and thoughtless pointing of
the camera but to a carefully designed 'chance process' as he
calls it, as he does when he has to determine the sounds to
be played in a piece of music. A chance process in which
personal preferences, the wish of himself as composer, as
photographer, to control the result, has been systematically
thwarted. He would, nevertheless accept the results, whatever
they may be, beautiful or ugly according to accepted canons,
as something to be liked, something to be learnt from, a fresh
view of what constitutes 'music', 'art', or 'reality'. A
different view of St. Ives. Not the one we remember, or invent,
when we think of the place.

The technique of doing something by chance (which I was learning
from the paragraphs, before each of his published writings,
describing exactly how it was composed) requires a carefully
chosen <u>system</u> of numbers, letters, or the like, with which
to denote all the possibilities one is leaving 'open to chance'.
It also requires a <u>source</u> of specific numbers, letters, or
whatever one is using, that are completely uninfluenced by any
bias, so that the results are picked out of the whole range of
possibilities in a completely random way. Random selection,
speaking mathematically, is that in which each choice is
uninfluenced by any other. In a row of random numbers eg
717882961434502103882944639636956001163488940884563664262636
each number has an equal chance of being any of the numbers
0 to 9 regardless of what comes before or after it. That is
why there are quite a number of repeats, when the numbers are
chosen without bias, whereas, in a row of numbers chosen to
fit one's IDEA of 'randomness' there may well be no repeats.
To eliminate all repeats is to impose pattern, idea.

My 'system of numbers' with which to denote all the possibilities

for photographing 'St. Ives' was a tourist map of the town. As
I was interested in seeing what chance photography would produce
in place of the 'typical' views in picture postcards and
holiday snaps I decided to restrict it to the most picturesque
part of the town: the neck of land connecting to 'the Island'
upon which are most of the fishermans cottages and which forms
the background to the harbour. My 'system' consisted of 10000
points on this part of the map at the intersections of a
100 by 100 grid. As soon as I saw the shape of this grid I
had visions of chance points landing on the beach or in the
sea, or inside someone's house. Wherever there was a chance-
selected point I'd be obliged to go, and take a photograph,
however difficult, embarassing, or 'untypical of photography'
it might be. And however much it might be 'not like me' to
do a thing like that. The St. Ives pictures were, I think,
my first chance process. Since then I have experienced many.
I've learnt, in all this, that this aspect of being driven, by
one's 'promise' to accept the results whatever they may be, is
perhaps the greatest fascination, though it can at times leave
one very exposed. It is the reality, the actual experience,
of being driven outside of 'oneself', one's idea of what one
likes, or dislikes, of 'who one is'. It is the process of being
exposed to parts of life that are inaccessible to one unless
one's preferences are given up. It is being put in touch with
aspects of life that are beyond the range of one's habits and
one's skills.

How to pick, from all the points on my imaginary grid, the ten
I planned to take? As I had no table of random numbers with me
I looked around for something in the environment itself which
permitted the selecting of ten points randomly from the ten
thousand. I found it in the church close to the lifeboat house:
a list of the dates of the various clergymen who had been in
office there since Elizabethan times. I copied out the last
two figures of each date and found there were enough numbers
to select five of my ten points. So I used the same set in
reverse order to select the other five, a slight departure
from true randomness which today I'd avoid. I realised that
the ten points, alone, did not suffice to determine what to

A map of St Ives, showing camera positions and the direction from which each photograph was taken

photograph. I'd need some way of randomizing not only the
location of the camera but its direction too. As time was
getting short I did this very crudely by allocating the compass
directions (I assumed North was at the top of the map) in the
sequence NSEWNSEWNS to each of the ten photos.

photo O
Taken before the chance photos to show the area of St. Ives
where they were to be taken, and as an example of a 'typical'
holiday view.

photo 1

For this and the other chance photos I was obliged to be
seen photographing obviously 'odd' views and experienced, for
the first time, the slight embarrassment of so doing. This
turf accountant's shop, which does not correspond to my notion
of such a place, or to my notion of 'St. Ives', is perhaps the one
that reveals most of that mass of experience we ignore, or cannot
assimilate consciously for want of any 'idea' or 'stereotype'
capable of including it.

photo 2
The first of several photos in which I had to stand ignoring
'prettier' views behind me to take what looked like ridiculously
close-up shots of seemingly dull walls etc.

photo 3
The chopping of the windows, and the slightly provocative
arrangement of rectangular areas in this photo, would suggest
to me now that it was done deliberately like this, to hold
attention, if I did not know it was done adhering to the chance
process as closely as possible.

photo 4
While taking this one I was beginning to feel the experiment
was a mistake. I'd have preferred the envisaged adventure of
having to knock on a door to say that I was obliged to take
a photo of, say, the inside of a house, because the chance
process had led me to that spot. (That accident did not
occur.) To take this photo, for which I had to stand alongside someone's house and direct the camera <u>along</u> a wall
instead of <u>at</u> it, felt like something too trivial to be
tolerated. Its amazingly difficult, for me at least, to do
something that is so bereft of any purpose that is self-
evident, or easily explainable to bystanders. Although the
camera did not show it, some of the photos were taken with
other holiday-makers at my elbow: for others, like this one,
there was nobody in sight and I was almost tresspassing.

photo 5
I'd looked at this signboard several times before as it was
near to where we were staying. It is something of an intended
'sight' in itself: a 'recognisable point of interest' such
as a guide might point out.

photo 6

For this photo the chance process put a point on the water
in the harbour. I should have obeyed it and swam out with
the camera, or hired a boat. As I was short of time, by
this (the points being quite far apart and the whole process
taking longer than I'd expected), I compromised by directing
the camera at the chosen point from the nearest spot on the
quay. This seems to have resulted in what is very close to
a 'composed' holiday snap. I'm always impressed by the way
in which, given a thing to photograph, it is so very
difficult to stop oneself conforming to some preconceived
notion of composition (eg eighteenth century landscapes
or Dutch interior paintings) every time one aligns the
viewfinder. The VIEW finder! A view, it seems, is not what's
there, what one's eye is capable of looking at and noting, but
a MEMORY of what others have done in composing what they saw?

photo 7

Perhaps the oddest photo in itself - half a car and a bit of
a house. Who would ever take such a picture? Some years later
my sister saw these slides and recognised this house as the
one her family had rented when they went to stay at St. Ives.
After many such seemingly spooky coincidences, arising from
chance processes, I have begun to be surprised not at their
occurrence but if, by chance, they do not occur. It seems to
me now that such unexpected connections exist between many of
the features of life we thought to be unconnected. Our
everyday perceptions are so narrowed by immediate purpose
and intention as to hide from us most of the connectiveness of
life. Deliberate chance processes break out of this a little
by obliging us to pay attention to what we are normally
incapable of noticing. Is that it?

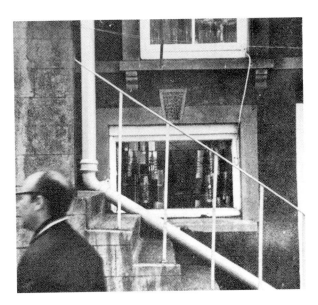

photo 8
Another close-up of a wall which, had I not known its origin,
I'd say was the work of an artist-photographer intent on
drawing attention by deliberate disregard of a recent convention
in how to 'compose a picture'.

photo 9
Again, though not a tourist's view of things, the chance process
seems to have led to the kind of composition reminiscent of
what some artists might well contrive.

photo 10
This last chance photograph is missing. The accident of losing
it gives us the opportunity of looking at something I did not
expect at all while taking the photographs: an image of St Ives
that leaves everything to the imagination; or else an image of
the frame, or idea, of 'a photograph' free of content.

Looking now at these photographs, eight years later, I doubt
if they are at all what John Cage would have done. For one
thing they embody only a part, the most managable but least
adventurous part, of his notion of chance composing. They
are an example of what I'd now call 'systematic' chance
processes: those in which there is a limited set of possibilities out of which a few are selected randomly. The more
adventurous kind of chance is what John Cage calls 'indeterminacy': the giving-up of all idea of what may result, as in his
musical piece 4' 33" (four minutes and thirty-three seconds in
which the performer makes no sounds from the musical instrument
and in which whatever sounds occur spontaneously in the hearing

of the audience comprise the music). But, even if John Cage
had himself decided to take photographs of St Ives, or if
anyone else but me had done so, trying to see the effect of
chance, the results might have been very different. They
would be different because, at the scale of 'the initial
decisions' (in my case: which part of St Ives to photograph,
how many to take, when to do it, how to organise the chance
process) there are still many many personal preferences to
be expressed, inevitably. But what matters, I think, is not
that the process, at its general level, remains intentional after
all, but that, at the scale of what are normally taken to be
the main decisions, intention is given up. Given that, there
appears enough of an opening for life, as we fail to predict
and to remember it, to enliven what we do.

For those who attended my talk, which included other things
besides this, here is a small quotation from John Cage's
Lecture on Nothing, which I recited. It is chosen by chance
using numbers taken from the dates of the St. Ives clergymen:

> It is not irritating to be where one is. It is only
> irritating to think one would like to be somewhere
> else.

References: The Lecture on Nothing appears in John Cage's
book Silence (Wesleyan University Press, Middletown,
Connecticut, 1961; Marion Boyars, London, 1971). A Year from
Monday is from the same publishers, 1967 & 1968 respectively.

composing by chance

In 1978 Chris Crickmay invited me to describe and demonstrate
chance processes in art and design to the people attending
an open workshop at the Whitechapel Gallery in London. I put
the essence of what I had to say on the poster which could
also be used as a work sheet. To show that chance composing
is not incompatible with traditional ideas of order I set out
the poster symmetrically and left the sequence of statements
and the selection of stencils and typewriter face to be determined by random number. I wanted to demonstrate that the
use of chance is not a hapazard action but is in its own way
precise.

once you've decided the composing process stick to
it, accept what comes

COMPOSING

HINTS FOR EASY COMPOSING
BEGIN WITH YOUR FEELINGS AND STRONG CONVICTIONS A-
BOUT WHAT YOU ARE COMPOSING / CHOOSE SOME SOURCES
TEXTS PLACES PEOPLE ETC RELEVANT TO THESE FEELINGS
THEN USE CHANCE PROCESSES

not just music : anything

poems plays novels journeys days lives pages films
radio-programs meals walks holidays philosophies g
ames concerts laws welfare medicare last rites any
thing that has to be organised before one can expe
rience it

BY CHANCE

35494 25220 91424 94750 70750 97663 18316 16741
50617 01404 78331 76908 68195 18714 28695 56066
21108 23021 31950 37840 33674 81877 92490 34588

WITH CHRIS JONES

108

This process, or something like it, occurred in the composing of
several of the essays and is described within some of them. Other
chance processes, perhaps closer to that described on the previous
page, are outlined here.

Choosing the quotations before each section:
First I chose authors from whom I'd learnt something during the
time when the essays were written and related one author to each
section. Then I took one or more books by each and used random
numbers* to select a page and a line (and also a book where there
was more than one). Lastly I chose a few lines of text in which
the line occurred to make evident the thought of which the line
is a part. For two of the quotations these chance-selected lines
seemed to lose significance out of context so I searched for
similar pieces of text which could stand independently. The
opening quotation is from an author from whom I'd learnt before
the essays were written and was selected in the same way. The
titles of the sections were selected similarly, as described on
page vi. Quotations, titles and photos were positioned by chance.

Choosing the illustrations before and after each essay:
The photographs are from colour slides I made during the time
when the essays were being written and the xerox pictures are from
objects found at chance-locations in Zurich and London. At first
I tried to consciously choose one photograph to match each essay-
title and one xerox picture to match each of the essays for which
there was an empty page left at the end. However I found myself
getting more and more dissatisfied with these choices, perhaps
because I was drawn into over-interpreting the titles and the
essays. There seemed to be too much of the essays, and of myself,
in what I was doing, and too little of the world. Eventually took
a slightly different selection of photographs and xerox pictures,
in about equal numbers, excluding those that had been chosen for
a particular essay but might not fit others, and used random
numbers to determine where each was to go. Although nervous of
this producing juxtapositions which might worsen rather than
improve the book I found that I liked the chance-positioning
better. It seems fresher, less heavy. I did however change an
essay title to avoid a juxtaposition that I did not like. The
ruled paper on page 242 was included because I originally ex-

pected it to accompany the essay "some reflections on chance"
with its references to determinism and because I wanted to include somewhere in the book the pure beauty of such designs.
The letter shapes on page 190 were drawn by Joel Fisher from
the accidental shapes found in the minute hairs in rag paper
and were originally selected to illustrate this essay. I
found the illustration by fixing a point in my room using
random numbers for the directions x,y, and z and taking the
nearest object to that point which could be xeroxed. The T-shirt
on page 218 was found in the same way as were other objects that
I did not use. Most of the other xeroxed objects were found by
picking what I saw at pre-specified places (fountains in Zurich)
or pre-specified times (on journeys in London). I decided to
include the frames of the colour transparencies when I noticed
how they drew my attention and how they kept the photographs
from too close an association with particular essays. The photographs of windows and window poems at the start and end of the
book were chosen deliberately when I noticed how well they related to the last paragraph of the preface. The opening photograph is from a colour slide chosen because it was made before
the essays were written.

This account, written after the event, makes it seems simpler
than it was. It took me weeks. The most difficult bit was
choosing, and rejecting, various sources of words and pictures
until some were found which in some indefineable way felt right
and likely to lead to happy accidents. Trying to imagine the
results, perhaps the main skill in conscious designing, under-
mines the confidence, in life, that is the basis of design-by-
chance. These examples are of course rather limited and circum-
scribed, hardly 'pure design'. I've yet to see an example of
real indeterminacy in visual design, equivalent to John Cage's
'silent' piece of music. It's difficult, very, to think how
and where to begin such an attempt. Perhaps the spatial world
is not as free as the temporal? Or is that a false distinction?...
This wasn't meant to be an essay. Just a note.

* One source is A Million Random Digits with 100,000 Normal
Deviates, The Rand Corporation, The Free Press, Publishers,
Glencoe, Illinois, 1965. "This book is the classic as far as
random numbers go." S.P.

some reflections on chance

an exchange of letters with David Miller

August 10, '78

Dear Chris,

Have just come across some reflections on <u>chance</u> in the composer Iannis Xenakis' book <u>Formalized Music</u> (pp. 204-5, 206), which I find interesting; wd. be interested to see a response from you if you have time & interest. Here are the passages:

"We know...that if an element of chance enters a deterministic construction all is undone. This is why religions and philosophies everywhere have always ~~driven~~ driven chance back to the limits of the universe. And what they utilized of chance in divination practices was absolutely not considered as such but as a mysterious web of signs, sent by the divinities (who were often contradictory but who knew well what they wanted), and which could be read by elect soothsayers. This web of signs can take many forms — the Chinese system of I-ching, auguries predicting the future from the flight of birds and the entrails of sacrificed animals, even telling fortunes from tea leaves. This inability to admit pure chance has even persisted in modern probability theory, which has succeeded in incorporating it into some deterministic logical laws, so that <u>pure chance</u> and <u>pure determinism</u> are only two facets of one entity...."

"....Epicurus, <u>who admits the necessity of birth at an undetermined moment</u>, in exact contradiction to all thought, even modern, remains an isolated case [footnote: Except perhaps for Heisenberg]; ~~~~ for the aleatory, and truly stochastic event, is the result of an accepted ignorance, as H. Poincaré has perfectly defined it." (What Xenakis seems to be pumping for here is the acceptance of uncertainty; & of indeterminism along with determinism.)

Anyway — if the above suggests anything to you, I'll be interested to hear yr. comments./Hope all is well.

love,
David.

David Miller was born in Australia and lives in London. His poem The Story was an inspiration for the essay Opus One, Number Two. The correspondence is reproduced with his permission.

August 10, '78.

Dear Chris,

Have just come across some reflections on chance in the composer
Iannis Xenakis' book Formalized Music*(pp. 204-5, 206), which I
find interesting; wd. be interested to see a response from you if you
have time & interest. Here are the passages:

"We know... that if an element of chance enters a deterministic
construction all is undone. This is why religions and philosophies everywhere have always driven chance back to the limits
of the universe. And what they utilized of chance in divination
practices was absolutely not considered as such but as a mysterious web of signs, sent by the divinities (who were often
contradictory but who knew well what they wanted), and which
could be read by elect soothsayers. This web of signs can take
many forms -- the Chinese system of I-Ching**auguries predicting
the future from the flight of birds and the entrails of sacrificed
animals, even telling fortunes from tea leaves. This inability
to admit pure chance has even persisted in modern probability
theory, which has succeeded in incorporating it into some
deterministic logical laws, so that pure chance and pure
determinism are only two facets of one entity..."

"...Epicurus, who admits the necessity of birth at an undetermined
moment, in exact contradiction to all thought, even modern,
remains an isolated case (footnote: Except perhaps for Heisenberg.);
for the aleatory, and truly stochastic event, is the result of
an accepted ignorance, as H. Poincaré has perfectly defined it."
(What Xenakis seems to be pumping for here is the acceptance of
uncertainty; & of indeterminism along with determinism.)

Anyway -- if the above suggests anything to you, I'd be interested
to hear yr. comments. /Hope all is well.

love
David.

*Iannis Xenakis, Formalized Music, Indiana University Press, 1971.
**I Ching or Book of Changes, especially the Wilhelm/Baynes trans-
lation published by Routledge & Kegan Paul, London, 1968.

12 August 78

dear David

Nice to get one of your profound questioning letters again. I once
started to read a thick book by Xenakis but put it down when I
ran into what I felt was the rationality-first assumption that is,
I believe, the recurrent symptom of whatever is skew-iff about
this culture we are socially in but, I trust, in our beings,
each much wider-than. There are no regular words in my repetoire
for trying to say how I think it is, only for saying how its
taught to be. So I keep getting drawn into hyphens, and to
words like wider that do not come very close to embodying what
I'm trying to think?

But perhaps I was wrong about Xenakis. I hope so, as his life
sounds good. I dont know his music.

Chance. As you may guess I have a lot of thoughts and notes
stored away (I'd intended to write a book on chance processes)
so I welcome this opportunity to think these thoughts again, and
perhaps to get a little further towards the clarity I dont think
I've managed to reach.

The quotation from Xenakis:
Firstly I cannot imagine how anyone can seriously <u>want</u> or
intend to make 'a deterministic construction' : the idea of
trying to do this fills me with uncomprehension, what possible
satisfaction could there be in doing that? I imagine that it
would generate in oneself that dislike of what one is doing when
one catches oneself making a doodle of some utterly predictable
pattern, or when, lying ill, one gets maddened by the repeats in
the wallpaper? The next sentence 'This is why religions and
philosophies everywhere have always driven chance back to the
limits of the universe' suggests to me a totally different
process than that of making a deterministic construction. To try
to make an explanation of the universe, to try to explain experience, is surely different from composing a new piece of experience. I feel it would take many pages to sort out a mass of

logical muddle that is implicit in making this comparison......

I feel that in both composing and in philosophising the charm
and attraction of the apparent completeness comes of the presence
of that which lies outside the construct : the presence of oneself, one's mind, the composer or philosopher too, and the
inexplicable complexity of life? The completeness is an agree-
able contrast to that but surely not the elimination of that, of
the possibility of life outside the construction?

But I seem to be quibbling at the inconsistencies coming not so
much from Xenakis's thoughts but from the vocabulary he is
obliged to use because we so lack words for saying this kind of
thought in a way that rings true.

I like what he says about oracles and the mysterious meanings
and intentions of the gods, or of fate, or of 'chance' imagined
as being a god or fate, and note immediately that Ed*, in his
book The Philosophers' Game, makes the writers of the I Ching
propose that this oracle shall be so constructed that it is seen
to be pure chance, and not an external fate, so that the person
consulting it is enabled to see that the decision lies entirely
with him or her. The oracle providing only a changed viewpoint
that the person could not have got unaided and which allows a
chance of seeing one's own bias, or narrowness. Perhaps, if
Ed's right about this, the I Ching is a means of getting immediately the more balanced view of what one is doing that can
otherwise be got only by waiting a long time, eg when one puts
a piece of writing away for a year or so and later is able to
see it quite differently?

Although, in using the I Ching, I've often had what seem, at first,
to be magical coincidences, I've realised with much experience of
the book and of using chance in composition, and in living, that
what it does is to enable one to be aware of a mass of
connections, between all we experience, that is hidden by our
intentions. Its not that the oracle is uniquely the cause or

* Edwin Schlossberg & John Brockman, The Philosopher's Game,
Elm Tree Books/Hamish Hamilton, London, 1978.

trigger of what one then sees is happening : it is I'd say the
means of losing the engrossment in one's purposes and thoughts
that hides what is happening, makes one unable to look.

There is I'm told a new school of mathematicians that denies
the logical laws of statistics to which Xenakis refers. The
most incredible of these laws, to me, is the one saying that, no
matter how many heads you toss in a row, the chance of getting
yet another head is still fifty-fifty. The law is obviously true
for imagined coin-tossing, in which a pure Platonic kind of chance
is assumed to be possible (ie one in which there can be no
physical connection whatever between one toss and the next), but
for any actual tossing, or other random-generating process, how
can one be absolutely sure that the connection between two events
is zero? Obviously one cannot. It is interesting that random
number tables are recognised by mathematicians to be what they
call pseudo-random because the process by which they are calculated, though intentionally very complex, is not completely
impossible to describe. The tables of random numbers are close
to being unpredictable, ie such that there is no connection
between numbers, so you cannot tell what the next will be by
studying the previous ones. To get the feel of what mathematical
randomness is like try writing out twenty numbers, single-figure
numbers from 0 to 9, in a row, before comparing what you have
done with the row I will copy onto the next page from a random
number table.

What Xenakis says about the laws of chance being deterministic
seems to me to be wrong : the law I quoted above surely does
posit pure chance?

I did not know that Epicurus had made that so fascinating statement about the moment of birth being undetermined but I like it
very much. The replies that astrologers give to the criticism
that birth is surely the moment of conception, not separation
from the mother, seem very weak, especially when you realise that
their trade would be difficult or impossible if they had to
accept the moment of conception. I've always felt that the image
of time as a thing, or as a line along which we move, is

inadequate, misleading, and feel its likely that esp etc is
mysterious only if one holds to our probably grossly wrong view
of time, or even the word itself, which seems to confuse rather
than clarify.

Of course I agree completely with Xenakis when he calls, as you
say he does, for acceptance of uncertainty along with determinism.
That is the whole point, I'd say, the religious belief in the
bounded nature of what we know and in the coherence, but not the
determinism, of what we do not.

Here is the string of random numbers:
22985951665490461995
The repeats surprise many people as does the absence from a short
string like this of some of the numbers, in this case 3 and 7 are
absent.

There is a big difference, which John Cage acknowledges, and makes
much of, between the results of a deliberately chosen chance
process (which all fall unpredictably WITHIN a chosen range of
possibilities) and the results of choosing to make something
that is indeterminate, as is his piece 4' 33", a duration (four
minutes, thirty three seconds) in which any sounds that occur
are accepted as music. In the second case there is a genuine
giving-up of control of what is to happen but in the first there
is only the widening of its range, keeping still to pre-set
limits. Cage's dislike of recordings (he seems not to count a
replay of a performance as music at all), and much of what he
writes, suggest that the true use of chance is outside the range
of "chance processes which are meant to be obeyed exactly". In
some or all of his compositions he does I think include disobedience of the self-imposed law of chance.

I could go on & on but I don't feel that I'm writing what we
have not discussed before, or getting close enough to the heart
of the matter, so I'll stop now.
All is a lot weller than it was.

                              love
                                 Chris

Here are some words chosen randomly, using random numbers to find
the page and the entry on the page, from the Shorter Oxford
Dictionary which contains about 75,000 entries:

respectively
olio   (stewpot or medley)
acceptable
ypsiloform   (y shaped)
jural   (relating to law or to rights & oblig-
                             ations)
predestinate   (to fix beforehand, or God doing so)
take   (to carry)
tent   (probe or dressing for a wound)
butt   (object of ridicule)
torment   (to agitate, shake or stir)

(LATER: I see now that the words & meanings chosen could be read
as magically relevant to our topic.)
I've tried to indicate the particular meaning chosen by random
process when there are several, or when the word is obsolete or
unfamiliar to me. All that is weak about using chance processes,
the lack of any presence of mind, is evident in this example, as
is the release from being in the hands of one person. I'll try
now to make a chance process that is not like that : one in which
the initial decision about where to choose the words from is a
felt and intended communication.*

I look at the books on my desk here seeking something I much like
and notice a book of Lorca's plays, in which are two announcements
to the audience that I love and which I asked to have read in
Spanish at points in my lecture in Argentina** to remind us of the
fantastic, so absent from the functionalist conception of design.
Here are ten words at random from the announcement read in

*   Actually, I remember now why I chose the Oxford Dictionary.
    I'd been listening to a poet reading poems a bit like Lax's,
    for 7 hours, & wished that his words had been less his choice
    & more the whole range of English words, : the experience for
    a listener would be that much more free, inspiring, releasive,
    strong, etc?
** See the essay "....in the dimension of Time."

120
Rosario:

audience
everywhere
becomes
dramatic
Silence!
fighting, fighting,
you
off
curtain

The repeated word, and the exclamation, occur in the text at the
points chosen randomly and are included in the list as an improvised disobedience of the self-imposed rule (of taking only one
word at a time).
Not very happy with this as a sample of the text I try another
kind of sampling, this time copying most of the line from which
each word came:

To the audience.
Everywhere walks and breathes the poetic creature
becomes visible reality
to set the dramatic example
Silence!
she is ever fighting, fighting,
You come in from the street.
He takes off his tall silk hat and it becomes illuminated
Grey curtain.

I find, as always, during the tiny drama of seeing what comes
next (which makes chance processes more interesting to operate
than to see the results of) that I lose all ability to react to
the words as a reader of the text I am composing. Even now,
minutes later, it has a not-from-me quality that is nice, and a
quality of nobody, me included, having been in on its composition, and so not yet having understood it, or 'read' it in the
sense of letting it form what meanings it can in my mind. The
writer becomes a reader, no more informed than any other. That,

I think, is very nice. Also the fact that anyone can do it, provided they have some sensitivity to the making of the initial decision of what to sample, what text or repetoire of items, and of what constitutes a unit of sampling. Obviously, in this not-so-hot example of mine, the letters and syllables, and even whole words, (which can include say a lot of the's a's of's etc) will not embody much of the reason why the text was chosen, so one has to decide the size of unit after a little trial and error, if sampling the text (to see what it is <u>like</u>) is one's intention.

I suppose using chance processes is no different in principle than for instance deciding to use the sonnet form. What it does is to enable one to operate one's intuitions at a larger scale than ususal, to compose using a far larger range of sources than is in one's memory, in detail, and is outside the capacity of one's word-producing-and-choosing process-skill to do itself. BUT, I find repeatedly, that after some hours/days/months of persistent and seemingly dumb-headed attempts at composing thus, one's intuitive process of word-and-thought-making-and-choosing is much improved, more catholic, and one has learnt not to censor one's words etc and to accept as relevant much that one could not use before. eg my later plays, like Arch & 35 wishes*,were done with a using of almost any (no, not ANY, but with a more inclus-ive acceptance) remark or event going on in the room as I typed, whereas Superman came entirely from randomly chosen pages of texts in mechanical obedience to process such as I've used here for the dictionary and for the Lorca list of single words. Enough? That anyone can write a single word : that's the real marvel.

*35 wishes appears later as an essay. Arch, and Superman Has Had His Day, have appeared in the poetry/performance journal Interstate published in Austin,Texas, issues nos 6-7 & 12.

August 15, '78

Dear Chris,

I think what Xenakis means is that if chance follows laws, pre-
determined patterns, which can be codified by means of divination
tables (e.g. I Ching) then what is being named by "chance" is
only another version of cause & effect. Chance which is caught
up in a network of relations is meaningful in the sense of being
given human meaning.

The answer to this is perhaps that the meaning is that provided
by chance & when we accept it, it means our boundaries of mean-
ingfulness have been in fact extended. I believe this is another
way of putting the same thing you mean by: "It...enable(s) one to
operate one's intuitions at a larger scale than usual..."

What Xenakis may be leaving out of the picture, in regard to
I Ching & related sources, is the whole question of interpretation:
one must be open to meaning & one must also select. Interpretation -- not only being able to interpret but having to of
necessity -- belies determinism. The value of such things as
I Ching may be that they can provide one with an opening onto a
horizon -- but in this sense chance would perhaps be a method
rather than a law?

                                        love
                                        David.

designing designing

Les Belady asked me to speak at a conference on the design
of computer software in 1978. The paper was originally
published under the title 'Designing as a Creative Activity'
in Infotech State of the Art Report; Structured Software
Development (edited by Peter Wallis) by Infotech, Maidenhead,
Berkshire, 1979. It also appeared under the present title in
Design Studies, volume 1 number 1, July 1979, pages 31-35.

This version is photocopied directly from the original typescript because I was attempting to communicate the process
of composing it and this is more evident there than in any
edited copy. Like some of the other essays appearing here it
was written by a process of typing 'camera-ready' pages directly out of mind, with some notes but no previous draft.
The process was carefully plannned but the content not. I
have found that this is not as difficult as it sounds (it's
certainly quicker) and it greatly alters what one writes as
well as how. It is more like speaking in that each word or
phrase inspires the next and what has been said cannot be
recalled once it has been uttered. I permit myself the use
of liquid paper eraser or even to start a page again, but
once a page has left the typewriter it cannot be changed.
It's published. Once it's typed it's published.

This essay was my first with 'prepared pages' in which sub-
titles, quotations, and the lengths of paragraphs are decided
(partly by choice, partly by chance process) before starting
to type. In this way the 'page one problem', or 'how to begin?', a recurrent difficulty when writing for strangers,
is avoided. All one has to do is to invent text to connect
the titles and quotations fixed in advance, trusting in the
process.

OUTLINE OF THE PAPER

The evolution of hardware (craft processes)

Conscious design of hardware (design by drawing)

The designing of intangibles (system desiging, software designing etc)

Design thinking (rational and intuitive)

Designing the design process (designing designing)

Design process control (five criteria)

Design process reviews (changing one's mind as one learns)

Divergent design processes (exploring the situation)

Transformational design processes (perception of problem/solution
                                                    interdependancy)

Convergent design processes (limits, alternatives, evaluations etc)

The essential point of my paper is that to invent something
new, and to bring it into being, is to change not only one's
surroundings but to change oneself and the way one perceives,
to change reality a little perhaps?
Thus the design process is one of devising and experiencing
a process of rapid learning about something that does not
yet exist by exploring the interdependancies of problem and
solution, the new and the old.

A question : is it necessary, or even possible, to understand
complelety the complexities of product and of its operation
when one is designing?

128

DESIGNING AS A CREATIVE ACTIVITY

Some years ago I wrote a book about designing : it was meant to
be my goodbye present to the subject, which I then proposed to
retire from after twenty years or so. I thought I had been in it
long enough and I was beginning to feel that it was not such a
creative or liberating activity as I had once fancied it to be.
In fact I was beginning to see design not so much as a process
of creation as a process of control, a way of fixing things, in
the drawing office, that would be much better left to the decision
of those whose lives were being conditioned by the shape and
form of man-made-things. But, having written the book, there
was no escape: I am continually being drawn back, from the
activities to which I tried to move, to give talks like this
one to audiences who apparently like to hear about the subject
from one who has been in it yet not entirely of it, part enthus-
iast, part skeptic.

However I did escape from designing for long enough to learn
something from the other arts, the time arts like film, poetry,
music and theatre, to which I became attracted. In particular
I learnt a lot from the composer John Cage and began to copy his
methods of composing by chance, giving up deliberate control of
the result. Another lesson learnt from him is that, if you want
to preach, the best way is by example. Everything John Cage does
is, as far as I can see, an example of what he recommends. So,
now that I am asked to write this summary of some of the main
aspects of 'how to design', I am reluctant to do so unless I can
make the paper itself an example of the methods I am to describe.
How to do that?

Looking for a clue as to how to begin, how to initiate a pleasant
flow of thought and words (pleasant for both of us, reader and
writer, I trust?) I examine closely the very clear instructions

provided by Infotech for speakers at the conference. The first
instruction, which had to be completed three weeks before sending
the paper, is to provide a short list of major topics,"10-12
subject headings". I provided ten. Another instruction calls
for a written paper of minimum length 3000 words. I calculate
that this would take about ten pages of typing so I immediately
decide to accept these two instructions as determinants of both
the length and the form of the paper : I take out ten blank
sheets intending to write exactly one page on each of the ten
topics. At this point I am in much doubt of the feasibility,
or even the wisdom, of taking such arbitrary decisions, but
I persist, trying to adopt the attitude of 'trusting the process',
the intuition, which tells me that this will turn out alright
even though at this moment I have no evidence that it wont be
a flop.

Next I realise that, though often in the past very attuned to
the subject, and full of words ready to come out, today my mind
is not on it at all. I am still thinking of some quite different
matters that have this week demanded attention and I cant see
any way of getting my thoughts about design back into the
forefront of my mind without a lot of tiresome re-reading and
note-making. And there is not time for that : the paper has to
be posted tomorrow. So I decide that I need a quickly-accessible
source of variety on each of the ten topics, something to get
me going immediately, something to react to. The most accessible
source I have is the book I wrote and my favourite way of consulting a book is by chance process, using random numbers to decide
the page and the sentences to read. I have often found that
an amazingly small number of sentences, picked in this unbiassed
way, and studied carefully, gives much of what one can learn by
reading the whole text. This paper, I decide, will include one
sentence from each of the chapters to which my ten titles refer.
And each section of it will consist of whatever that quotation
brings to mind, now that I am thinking about the designing of
computer software.

Looking now at the first quotation, which is about the evolution
of the complex and beautiful shapes of farm waggons by craftsmen

who knew exactly what to do, in detail, but seldom knew why,
I am reminded of what might, by now, be called the collective
folk-art of writing computer programs, an art in which many
collaborate in an evolving work that is seldom seen and understood as a whole by any individual. To make my process of
composing this paper as much like that as possible,I decide
to pick all the quotations, randomly, before starting to
write, and to type each quotation at a randomly chosen point
on its page before writing anything else. Now all I have to
do is to think of words that will fit my thoughts exactly into
the spaces before and after each quotation. This seemingly
irrational decision feels to me as if its going to add some
difficulty, but also a little excitement, to the process of
writing, as I tailor my words to fit the spaces decided in
advance. Certainly this design of the composing-process will
get me over the writer's perennial difficulty of 'how to get
going' while being only too aware of the many objections that
readers might have to any thought that comes to one's mind, and
being equally aware that any false move may upset the structure
of the paper as a whole and drive one back to square one (a
familiar enough place to all designers, as well as writers).
With my arbitrary design of the form of the paper to adapt
myself to I will have little time or need for these worries.

Not having anything else to say before turning to the first
new page and subtitle I decide to pick at random an illustration
from my book to fill up the rest of this page:

Fig
1

THE EVOLUTION OF HARDWARE (craft processes)

I was asked, in this paper, to describe "how, in general, you
do it" ('it' being design) : how one creates THE NEW. And also
to say how one evaluates alternatives, how one formulates
requirements for a system without pre-judging how to do it, etc.
Before attempting to answer these modern questions, which
assume that the designing of man-made things is a wholly conscious process in the mind of one person, the chief designer,
it is helpful, I think, to look at the works of the past,many
of which, though of complex and coherent form, were not 'designed'
at all but were evolved over generations by slight modifications
made by craftsmen responding to the trials and errors of practical necessity in a social and physical situation that, by
modern standards, remained stable for centuries. It is also
helpful to think about the evolution of natural forms, a process
that is even slower, is probably more complex than anything we
do in design, and is even less a conscious process. And we,
with our ability to evolve and design things, tangible and
intangible, are, apparently, one of the results of this evolution. Its hard to believe.

My knowledge of craft evolution comes largely from the writings
of George Sturt, one of the few people to have practiced an
ancient craft and afterwards to have put his experience into
writing. Normally craftsmen are, perhaps of necessity, people
of few words,and often illiterate. He describes how, in making
a farm wagon, he relied on knowledge 'which was set out in no book':

> I knew that the hind-wheels had to be five feet two inches
> high and the fore-wheels four feet two; the the "sides"
> must be cut from the best four-inch heart of oak, and so on.

Yet the results of this 'mystery' as he calls it, this body of
knowledge 'residing in the folk collectively' is a precision, in
relating one part to another, and in relating the whole to the
slightest differences in needs and preferences of particular
customers, that now seems lost forever. Cybernetically, we
might say, there is hidden intelligence in seemingly blind
evolution. And a subtle flexibility.

THE EVOLUTION OF HARDWARE (craft processes)

I knew that the hind-wheels had to be five feet two inches
high and the fore-wheels four feet two; the the "sides"
must be cut from the best four-inch heart of oak, and so on.

(a "prepared page" as it was before the text was written)

CONSCIOUS DESIGN OF HARDWARE (design by drawing)

It seems that, traditionally, craftsmen used no sketches or
scale drawings. In fact the pictures which George Sturt
drew for his book are pathetic examples of inability to draw
and envisage in two dimensions, apart from the object itself.
But 'design-by-drawing' evolved, out of craftsmanship, perhaps
by putting together, on one sheet of paper, the curves and
templates used for recording cross-sections, and the like, which
could not be retained sufficiently exactly in memory alone.
Once discovered, this putting-together onto one sheet, into one
data structure as we'd call it, permitted many new developments
which were outside the scope of the dispersed intelligence of
craft evolution. For instance it allowed a jump in scale:

> Initially this advantage of drawing-before-making made
> possible the planning of things that were too big for a
> single craftsman to make on his own, eg large ships and
> buildings.

This advantage, together with others, equally great, comes of
giving up the craftsman's flexibility, his freedom to adjust
each part to fit the next and to fit the unique requirements of
each customer. Craftsmen are replaced by operatives obeying,
without knowing why exactly, the precise dimensions and tolerances
of a scale drawing, so that designers, a new class, are enabled to
organise the works of several operatives so that they will fit
together even though manufactured by people working at different
times in different places. Thus it becomes possible to switch
from piecemeal evolution, at the scale of the part of a design
which itself is largely stable, to the conscious changing of the
design as a whole, using a symbolic geometric model, the drawing,
to permit experiment that is not possible when changes are limited
to the product itself. What strikes me most,about this new
freedom to design instead of just evolve,is that it is obtained
at such high cost, the loss of the ability to adjust the shape
of things to reflect what makes life really human. There arises
a profound conflict between the geometric uniformity of what the
designers have understood and the barbaric ignorance of everything
non-visual that the scale drawing fails to represent.

THE DESIGNING OF INTANGIBLES (system designing, software
designing, etc)

The traffic problem (congestion, parking, accidents, etc) is
typical of the seemingly insoluble problems arising today when
the growth of designed products (eg vehicles, roads, carparks,
traffic signals),each designed in isolation by specialists,
creates enormous difficulties outside the range of what designers
and the drawing process can respond to. So now there exist a
number of new design methods that are intended to operate at the
scale of these problems, the scale of system, the scale of the
invisible and intangible patterns of experience and use.

> Unfortunately the information necessary to assess the
> feasibility of a new system proposal is scattered among
> many brains and many publications and some of it may
> have to be discovered by new research.

That reason is one of several that explain why these new methods
of designing at the scale of system are not yet very successful.
To solve the problems created by the specialization of the craft
process, its fragmentation into a growing number of professions
each highly specialized, requires more than a change in methods
of thinking and of modelling. It reqires an ability we do not
yet have : the ability to communicate fully and quickly across
the barriers that separate professions and which isolate their
thinking from the experience of users. Perhaps it requires the
disbanding of our tradition of separating planning from using,
and a return to much less specialized, and more integrated, forms
of responsibility and work. Certainly it needs some really
fresh thinking about how to use computers and communication media.
Our efforts so far to organise life at the scale of the system
seem to rely not on rethinking the aims and purposes and modes of
operation of activities like transport, education, medical
treatment, housing, telecommunications, etc. All we have done so
far is to homogenize : to force life to fit increasingly stand-
ardized systems that are simple to design but insensitive to how
it feels to use them. And our excuse, as professionals, as non-
persons, is 'I only work here'. It is clear to me that no big
change is possible till we change ourselves and our ideas.

DESIGN THINKING (rational and intuitive)

There is plenty of evidence, apart from what I have to say
about the inadequacy of our design methods and the over-
specialized way we work as professionals, that we inherit a poor
way of thinking about reality, a picture of the world, of life,
that fails to reflect the connections between things, and in
particular the connections between aspects of life which we
habitually divide into seeming opposites : art & science, theory
& practice, work & leisure, fact & opinion, etc. We have a
split view of life, a view that may well have been necessary to
the solving of physical problems, mechanically, but which has
now become the main obstacle to solving the problems created
by mechanization. In designing,this difficulty appears as
the separation of the rational from the intuitive, the practical
from the creative. But the briefest study of how the most
successful artists, engineers, scientists, etc work and think
suggests that they have one thing in common : they have found
ways of avoiding this split, of combining reason <u>with</u> imagination,
of being both creative <u>and</u> practical, of knowing when its
rational to be irrational and when its rational work by experience.
To reconcile what seem to be opposites, to resolve contradictions,
is the essence of design. And to do this one has to rely on one's
nervous system, one's uncontrollable inspiration, one's mind-body.

>The technique can be regarded as one of removing the
>social inhibitions that each person normally applies to
>his output during a conversation: it is a deliberate
>return to the illogical and 'ego-centric' talk of
>children that has been recorded and explained by Piaget
>(1959) and others.

That is a description of brainstorming, one of the new techniques
for deliberate, rational, stimulation of the irrational, the
seemingly crazy, the source of insight and originality. It is
the rationale for using the irrational. Equally, a description of
what is happening in a seemingly rational technique, like
classification, shows that it depends upon intuition, upon making
decisions with an inner confidence that cannot be justified by
reason.

DESIGNING THE DESIGN PROCESS (designing designing)

The new design methods (brainstorming, system engineering,
operational research, and many others) are not easy to use.
They very easily become uncontrollable and confusing so that
the designers get swamped in a mass of information, and a
rigidity of procedure, that prevents common sense, intuition,
and one's own abilty to think, from remaining in control. This
is because they are presented as what they are not : panaceas,
complete substitutes for thinking for oneself, for being responsible for what one is doing. The missing element is what I
call 'designing designing' : the conscious direction of part
of one's activity and energy, while designing, into the meta-
process of designing the process of design. At any point one
should be aware of 'what you are doing' and 'why'.

> A great advantage of the formal statement of a possible
> strategy is that everyone who is expected to put it into
> effect is able to contribute to the choice of methods
> and can see clearly how his own actions contribute to the
> whole.

The design process, or strategy, can be expressed as a program
or sequence of proposed techniques, each likely to generate the
answer to a question and enabling the next question to be posed.
Thus the design process is the designer's way of discovering
what he knows, and what he does not know, about this new thing
that he has promised to invent, and to integrate into the world
as it is. When the designer is a group of people, unused to
each other and to the problem, as is so often the case today,
the conscious attempt to continually design, and redesign, the
design process is an excellent way of seeking the kind of understanding of what is afoot, and willingness to do it, that is
so easily lost in working in a design team. The essential step
is to recognise that nobody, least of all the chief designer,
has,at the start,the knowledge to say how the design will turn
out,or even what the problem really is - how it will seem when,
eventually, everyone's intuitions become informed by the experience of having designed it. At he start one's intuition
is likely to be wrong, informed by what IS,but not by what is
to be conjoured into existence.

DESIGN PROCESS CONTROL (five criteria)

One of the most obvious ways of trying to improve one's designing
is to identify, and take steps to avoid, the causes of design
failure, the reasons why such a high proportion of new products
do not succeed (its said to be 4 out of 5). There is quite a
lot written by experienced designers about how and why design
blunders occur and how to avoid them,eg:

> The actions expected of the design team members must be
> those of which they are capable, in which they have
> confidence, and which they are motivated to carry out.

From such very obvious-seeming, but apparently easily-overlooked,
statements,by those who have learnt the hard way,I have compiled
a list of five most-common causes of failure and expressed these
as the following criteria to be applied when asking oneself
'is my design process adequate?' :

1. Identify the critical decisions (those which, if wrong, mean
certain failure, eg choice of objectives), and review these at
intervals using the best available advice.

2. Relate the cost (of design and research effort) to the penalties
for not doing it, trying always to identify the questions it is
supposed to be answering.

3. Match the design activities to the abilities, motivations,
and confidence of those expected to carry them out.

4. Before seeking the answer to any question assess the reliability
and relevance of the sources one intends to consult.

5. Always explore the interdependancy of the product and its
environment, ie assess the sensitivity of the supposed definition
of the problem to change when seen in the light of novel solutions.

A more detailed description of these criteria appears on pages
57 & 58 of my book Design Methods.

DESIGN PROCESS REVIEWS (changing one's mind as one learns)

One of the simplest ways to organise one's design thinking
and documentation is to keep three sets of papers for three
categories of thoughts and data : set 1 being for information
about the problem and attempts to analyse and understand it,
set 2 being for tentative solutions (which should always be
developed and noted at the moment of their occurence and
never inhibited in favour of more rational work; they can
also be usefully categorised as immediate improvisations,
new designs which fit the status quo, and more fundamental
solutions which call for considerable reorganization), set 3
being for spontaneous thoughts, feelings, doubts, hunches, etc
which may well conflict with what is in sets 1 & 2 and which
will be useful in periodic reviews of one's strategy, telling
one how one's mind and morale is reacting to the procedure
one has decided to follow. If one externalizes all these
kinds of thinking, instead of just experiencing them, one
has the beginnings of the meta-process with which to control
one's designing so that it does not get out of touch with
reality.(reality, in design, being as much one's suppositions,
imaginations, and feelings as it is one's picture of the
so-called 'real world'). Design process reviews should be
occasions when the contents of these three accumulating
results of what one has been doing are studied,compared,
pondered, slept-on, etc. In reviewing, and changing, one's
design process one tries to keep it sensitive, human.

> The new terminologies and procedures of designing and
> planning lose both their realism and their validity as
> soon as they cease to reflect the personal issues which
> matter most to the people who take decisions or are
> affected by them.

This means that, at any point, no matter how much has been
invested in what has been done so far, one retains the readiness to abandon anything that feels wrong, absurd, misguided,
etc, and to switch, at all costs, to what seems sensible and
right in the light of what one has just learnt.

DIVERGENT DESIGN PROCESSES (exploring the situation)

Divergence is polite word, borrowed from mathematics, for the
process of letting oneself become deliberately confused, uncertain, unworried, uninhibited, etc, in one's thinking about
what the problem really is and what kinds of solution are
relevant to it. As one is, in fact, more likely to be over-
sure, anxious, inhibited, narrow-minded etc in one's initial
assumptions about how to tackle the problem it is useful to
accept the discipline of some of the newer design methods
which are intended to help the designer to break out of
pre-conceptions and thus to be able to see the problem, and
its possible solutions, in a fresh light. There are methods
such as brainstroming and synectics, which help one to change
and widen one's point of view, and methods like observing
users (ergonomics) and rapid searching of literature which
get one out of the desk-bound mentality into some direct
contact with the people and situations one is supposed to be
trying to assist. Its obvious, once you think about it, that
no new thing, no originality or creativeness, is going to
emerge if one sticks rigidly to an orderly design process in
which one never gets in a mess, never loses touch with one's
pre-conceptions, never lets go of THE KNOWN. The first practical step, to this end, is to set aside the objectives, as given
by the sponsor, and to treat them as tentative guesses which
are likely to be revised once the design situation has been
explored. Equally, one sets aside one's own ideas of what is
relevant and what is not. Creativity is not so much having
good ideas as being willing to attempt what is unfamiliar,
being willing to change one's mind.

It may be useful to think of divergent search as being
a testing for stability, or instability, in everything
connected with the problem; an attempt to discover what,
in the hierarchy of community values, systems, products,
and components (and also in the minds of those who will
take critical decisions) is susceptible to change and
what are to be regarded as fixed points of reference.

Without this divergence, this rough-and-tumble, designing is
merely an ingenious perpetuation of the status quo, the self.

TRANSFORMATIONAL DESIGN PROCESSES (perception of problem-
solution interdependancy)

Many design situations do not call for a change in how one
perceives the problem, or in the kind of solution that is seen
as appropriate. They resemble the situation of the wagon
maker, the craftsman, sensitively assisting in a vast
collaborative process in which the creativity resides outside the conscious reach of any one designer, and which calls
for a selfless dedication. That attitude has been, perhaps,
the real strength of engineering, as it has been the strength
of Chinese art, Noh theatre, etc. Ego-free, modest, and
extraordinarily effective in the long run. But now, in the
new situation of partial breakdown of technology itself,
brought about by the unquestioned expansion of all feasible
technologies regardless of how harmfully they interact, we
seem to require a drastic change in how designing is done.
To be creative now is not to perpetuate technology but to
find new directions, to find ways of acknowledging, in the
development of the new, the interconnectedness, the coherence,
of life. Particularly, is this so, in the designing of new
means of communications, and of computing. Transformational
designing is the process of finding new points of reference,
while discarding the old, and out of this, an induced doubt,
a new skepticism, making a new picture of reality.

> Out of all this comes the general character, or pattern,
> of what is being designed, a pattern that is perceived as
> appropriate but cannot be proved to be right.

This is the new, and enlarged version of the 'flash of insight',
the eureka-feeling, that comes of finding a new way to perceive
the design situation as a whole, a perception in which the
conflicts, and apparent opposites, of an 'insoluble' problem
are resolved by finding a new kind of solution in which those
contradictions do not even arise. One cannot force one's mind
to hit upon such insights to order. But what one can do is
to plunge boldly, and intelligently, into the previous state
of divergent search, confident that, if one tolerates its
uncertainties, one's nervous system will do the rest.

CONVERGENT DESIGN PROCESSES (limits, alternatives, evaluations etc)

> One is the conventional <u>out-in</u> strategy, such as an
> architect may employ when proceeding from the external
> shape of a building to the arrangement of rooms within it.

That is a description of the customary design strategy in
professions like architecture and engineering where, until
recently, it has been both possible and desireable to rely,
for the general pattern, the organising idea, upon the
experienced judgement of one person, the chief designer. But
now, when the thing to be designed is often outside the
experience of anyone, particularly in its effects and interactions with other things, man-made and natural, the <u>out-in</u>
method is a recipie for failure, for perpetuating what is wrong.
in the situation as a whole. The strategy for converging on
the general form of the design is more likely to be right if
it begins with the details, the mass of seemingly conflicting
and irreconcilable requirements, and, out of this confusion,
seeks a new order. There are, in the repetoire of new methods,
several which are very helpful in the data-handling problems
of juggling with far more alternative sub-solutions than can
be held in memory, and these, as one would expect, make use
of computer programs.(eg AIDA, and morphological analysis).
However, it is likely that this <u>in-out</u> procedure, if relied
upon as an automatic pathway to originality, will turn out
to be as unhelpful as was the earlier reliance upon the back-
of-the-envelope-sketch, the design tool of the over-confident
chief. I suspect that the best designers, in the past as now,
have always used a personal mixture of these two approaches,
contradictory as they seem, and somehow found ways of getting
the advantages of each: speed, clarity, combined with detailed
realism.

Now, having come to the end of my ten pages of text to be
composed to fit titles and quotations pre-arranged upon the
page, I am wondering which of these strategies, and of the
others mentioned, I have managed to demonstrate in the writing?

SOURCES

The first quotation, about wagon making, comes from George
Sturt's book The Wheelright's Shop; Cambridge University
Press; London, 1923, which is a marvellous little book and
has remained in print since it was first published.

The other quotations are from my book Design Methods and
are the copyright of the publishers John Wiley & Sons; London,
New York; 1970. The specific methods, such as brainstorming,
synectics, AIDA, etc, mentioned in the paper, are descibed in
some detail in this book, which is a review of the newer
design methods and an introduction to the principles of design.

The photograph of a farm wagon is from the collection of the
Museum of English Rural Life at the University of Reading.
It is a South Midlands Spindle-sided wagon from Hailey,
Oxfordshire, built in 1838.

(The book by Jean Piaget, which was not given in the original
paper, is The Language and Thought of the Child, published
by Routledge and Kegan Paul, London, 1959.)

It seems clear that if I wrote to
you about something I would not be writing to you but for you
and therefore creating an object rather than trying to realize
a context where ideas could be experienced. Also, I would be
engaging in the peculiar emotional role of asking you to read
something not as a direct communication, but as a finished piece,
of which you could only be a passive observer. I am not interested in passivity at all and so the process of composing for me
is an active process to relate through the context of these
words how I think and therefore how I am thinking. The context
and the content are interacting and making me as present as I
can be without the alienating posture of describing an objective
reality — whatever that might be.

Edwin Schlossberg
For My Father

3
IT MUST GIVE PLEASURE

opus one, number two

In 1978 Tony Ward, one of the organisers of the Portsmouth
conference on design methods of 1968, invited the speakers
to re-assemble for another conference, ten years later. He
asked us to speak of our (probably changed) views of the
subject and of its relation to 'the real world'. The conference did not take place but some papers were written and
published in Design Studies. This paper appeared in Design
Studies volume 1 number 6 in October 1980 pages 373-7. I am
grateful to Butterworth Scientific Ltd (formerly IPC Science
and Technology Press Ltd) PO Box 63, Westbury House, Bury
Street, Guildford, Surrey GU2 5BH, for permission to reproduce
it here.

The paragraphs at the start of Part 1 and Part 2 were written
after the paper had been completed.

Part 1   The architecture of the Open University

My attempts, while thinking-at-the-typewriter, with the help
of various authors, to understand why design methods seem to
have failed, why industrial life seems to have failed, become
rigid, homogenized, inhuman. What's missing?
. . . .

Since 1968 I have found myself leaving most of what, up till
then, I had been doing. I left design methods, feeling that it
had become a rigid and inhuman activity, and I left academic
life, at the Open University, feeling that that too had become
rigid and inhuman. And now there are many critics of design
methods, as applied to architecture, who imply that the rigidity
came from the misconceptions of those, like myself, who foisted
mechanical ways of thinking onto the architectural profession,
which thus lost some of its freedom. The methods did not fit
the mind.

I do not want to continue this dispute. It would surely be
better to seek (in thinking about what we have experienced these
last ten years) not blame for what has gone wrong but some
responsibility for putting things right.

I chose this title 'The architecture of the Open University' not
because I have a lot to say against the way it is organized
(which I have) but because the title makes it evident that we
are now living on the other side of a revolution in industrial
life: the...

Just as I am thinking how to complete that sentence I am amazed
and delighted to hear, on the radio, something of a kind I've
never heard before:

> at a break in a concert a most un-announcer-like voice,
> presumably a member of the orchestra, sitting some way from
> the mike, says 'we will play the finale - opus one number
> two'

I am amazed because I can't recall any occasion when I've

noticed a broadcasting authority giving up, and thus making
visible, its normally hidden exclusion of anyone but those
with officially approved voices, and officially approved words,
from making any announcements. This control, absolute as it
usually is, is, if you think of it, the way in which all broadcasting organizations put limits to the public space which they
control. I'm delighted to have heard this tiny breakdown in
that homogeneity not only because it is an accidental blow for
freedom but because it immediately opened to the imagination an
utterly different, and far more human, kind of broadcasting that,
in the 50 or so years since the invention of radio, we have hardly
ever been allowed to experience. A radio in which the authority
is gone and we rely in the studio, as we do in conversation and
in most other occasions for talking and communicating, on impro-
vization and not on planning.

That little interruption, from whoever spoke those not-quite-
official words, has almost said what I was about to say about
the recent revolution in industrial life. The change from products to processes, from hardware to software, from architecture =
buildings to architecture = the way life is organized. The
Open University's buildings are a small and irrelevant part of
what it offers to students whereas the teaching programmes, and
the papers and broadcasts by which they are transmitted, together
with the odd corners of houses and technical colleges where the
learning takes place, are what the university consists of. The
change from university-as-place to university-as-procedure
(which can occur in almost any place) is the revolution I am
talking about.

The revolution-within-that-revolution, which has never happened,
but which is hinted at in that half-unofficial announcement, is,
to me, what is missing from design methods, from software designing, from architecture, from industrial life : humanity.
Industrial life, considered as a set of organised procedures,
excludes, at almost every point what broadcasting authorities
exclude from announcements : the freedom to act as a person and
not as a THING. Things, which are not expected to think for
themselves, being the model for professional behaviour. For

doing what you are paid to do. But to be a person is surely to
BE. We have somehow accepted, as normal, as "in the public
interest", that industrial life is to be organised to eliminate
all opportunities to be.

But I promised not to argue, to get angry, and here I am beginning to do that..........Is there any way to put things right?

It is now some hours since I put that question but no answer
comes.

The question is too difficult.

So I begin to consult some of the voices to which I have been
listening, during the years. Perhaps an answer may come,
unexpectedly, from another mind, if I sit here a little longer,
waiting. And typing out some words from an armful of books
taken from my shelves. Some of the books that have taught me
to look outside that world of methods; which once seemed larger
than it does today.

---

      you & I, we, already exist
      in this work. it has no doors.
      we already exist in it.

      without too great a fuss
      we have taken posession
      of the restaurants & cabaret of West Europe
      & we sing, eat & drink to your health.

Perhaps that one voice, David Miller's, is enough.

Enough to let us realise that to talk and think of the world as
something apart from ourselves is nonsense. We cannot be outside.

Though, I guess, our roles can limit us to small segments of the

world. So that it seems, as Tony Ward put it in his letter
inviting papers for this conference, that what's "actually done"
is "out there, in the world". But we are in the world. We are
the world. All of us. What is this paradox, this near-cert-
ainty that we are not alive to being alive?

A few days ago I read something (in the draft of a thesis on
design methods & architecture) which allowed me to recover much
of my old enthusiasm for the subject:

> the isolate is an abstract fiction: to understand reality
> is to see and understand things in their connectedness and
> in their interpenetration, one to the other.

The thesis is by W H Nichols. What I suddenly recaptured was
the conviction that, whatever may have become of design methods
in recent years, the original intentions of those of us who tried
to improve design processes, ten or more years ago, was to respond to the connectedness of everything. To cease splitting life
into fragments, particularly when it is people and the experience
of life that is being fragmented. I realised that the intention
of the new methods, (mine anyway, and I think its true of many
others) was to overcome the limitations of professional procedures in all the design professions. Their inability to
respond to life itself, which was becoming the object of design,
as the extent of what is man-made grew and grew. To make what
Thomas Khun has called a paradigm-shift, in the nature of
designing. To change the objectives, the criteria, the procedures. To abandon specialisation, which pre-supposes that
products, buildings & the like can be adequately designed by
separate groups of professionals, in isolation, leaving the
connections between designed things and what exists to take
care of itself.

I think now, when I reconsider this notion, that what has happened is this:

Interconnectedness was accepted as a fact.

Design processes have somehow been adapted to permit the
integrated design of building-complexes, shopping precincts,
hypermarkets, multi-storey hospitals, urban motorways etc

But the paradigm-change was resisted. We still have
specialised design professions, and we still have the old
idea that what is being designed is "objects". The designers
persist in acting as if they themselves are objects and the
people whose lives are being shaped by this objective process
are being treated as objects. Without minds of their own.

We have yet to face up to the changes needed in everyone's roles,
self-images, procedures, and ways of life, if the interconnectedness for which we design is to include the most difficult part
of the problem:

what makes us people, and not objects, is that we <u>are</u> the
interconnections..............as objects we interconnect to
a large degree, but as minds we interconnect far more than
that.

So, if, as we have done, we design for interconnection only at
the object level (limiting ourselves to what can be calculated
and neglecting what can only be imagined, and felt, but not
measured), we are bound to create a way of life which is experienced as inhuman. Homogenized architecture : homogenized milk.

we will play the finale - opus one, number two

At last, at last, this piece of writing begins to feel good.
Begins to be a nice process. I'm beginning to enjoy doing it.
Reading it? That's another matter. Unpredictable.

What can we learn from architecture? The old architecture.
Buildings, places.............places to be. As described by
P'ei Ti, writing a thousand years ago, in China:

154

```
            In front of the balcony,
                as the expanse of water
                fills with ripples,
            The solitary moon
                goes wandering without pause.
            From the depth of the valley
                the cries of the monkeys rise;
            Borne by the wind
                they reach me in my room.
```

The building itself is barely mentioned. Yet its presence is
felt. What is described, recreated, is the experience. Of being
there, and of what else is there. The state of mind. Consisting
of all these things. This, this so delicate awareness, is closer,
I suppose, to "life", to what I'm now calling the new architecture, the architecture of being, of being here, of making the
connections, for oneself. ?

When we design the interconnectedness what becomes of this?

The architecture of the open university, of industrial life.
The architecture of process. Of life as process. As process
designed.

```
            at this point:
            viola music.
```

I'm still quoting from David Miller's poem. The Story.

```
            to question the term "unit" is to
            question the term "totality"
            & I question it.
            no one knows what is meant by
                                    "perception".
```

---

opus one, number two

the new architecture

the architecture of all that's made

we speak for ourselves

as the architects

of how we live

when can we begin?   all of us

That was not meant to be a poem. It was meant to be a list.
A list of some of the nicer thoughts to be extracted from what
has appeared so far, in this piece. From what has come to mind.

Briefly, what seems to have happened, is this:
The new methods, which once seemed as if they could, and would,
be used to make designing more sensitive to the ways in which
life's now lived, have instead been used, if they have been used
at all, to make it less so. In widening the field of what is
designed we have retained the control that a craftsman exercises
over his work, the artist of his medium. Forgetting that the
medium has changed its nature. That, in a widened designing,
we begin to be the medium ourselves. And we dont need to be
made, to be designed. We already ARE. How then, in widening
design, are we to share control, to share the role of architect?
I know very well that that question can be said to be in the
realm of politics, not architecture. Of course its impossible
to fit into the conventional notion of what architectue IS.
The old conception has to go. Beautiful as it was, in front
of the balcony. The paradigm has changed. And what we see
so far is very ugly.

......true beauty is forced far off, and retires to distant places.

```
          we already exist in this work.
          it is not context.  there is no containment.

          a wilderness.
          a house.
          a City.
          in the work our faces (& the faces of our friends)
          assume a reckless humour,
          I
          love them, the glass
          floods with light.
```

A light used to flood, in the fifties, when we thought about
design-as-process, about all designing as one process, a collective work. The same light flooded, in the thirties, and before, when they talked of function, function as liberation from
self-expression, from arbitrary imposed forms, from tyrrany,
the tyrrany of the old, kept alive, as imposed forms, long after
the life those forms reflected, and imposed, was over. It
was a light. Where is the light now?

```
we will play the finale
though its not a finale
more like a new start
opus one, number two
the architecture of the open university
the architecture of
                of
```

It hasn't happened yet. And yet its surely here, already,
in its essentials, in ourselves, and in what we have made, in
the accidents, the implications, of what has been done, to extend life. Just as all the words to be written are present,
potentially, in the making of pens, paper, presses, computers,
and the like. So many houses, implicit in the brick. These
words. These people.

What's absent is ourselves. Hiding in our roles. Here we are.

Not many of us are members of the Open University. Not many of
us are architects, or engineers, or politicians, or announcers,

Why not? Why are we excluded, from being? The open university
could have been for everyone. Perhaps it still can. Like the
phone.

It needs a discipline, obviously. A discipline of process. An
architecture, of being. A way to share control. Here we are.
We've got the wrong disciplines. (These staccato sentences:
they were written very slowly. Is that a hint?) We need a
little recklessness.

How to put things right?

Part 2   Opus one, number two

More thinking-at-the-typewriter in which I realise that, in
attempting to change the processes of design, in trying to
increase the scale, the scope, of the man-made, we failed
to change the aim, the goal. Design-as-process, design at
the scale of being, does not have a goal. Its non-instrumental.
Its a question of living, not of planning life-not-yet-lived.
Design without a product. The idea seems nonsense if applied
to designing by professionals. But, seen as part of an
historic shift from product-thinking to process-thinking,
isn't it what we overlooked? Designing disappears : becomes
a way of using, an enlivening of how we live. There is no
outcome. Its a question of being, without stop
. . . .

OPUS ONE, NUMBER TWO

the architecture of process
the architecture of what is happening
the architecture of being

A time for relearning.
Ten years later we realise that, as makers of methods, we have
got lost.
The situation created by what we did, and by the reactions to it,
does not allow us to proceed. We are obliged to pause, to rethink, to discover what went wrong. The obstacles that now
confront us give us the opportunity to relearn, to develop, to
grow. To give up whatever it was that led us astray. Let us
use the opportunity, this conference, to do that. What we did
before is finished. We cannot repeat, we have to change. We
are in a muddle. Let's begin with ourselves in trying to sort
it out. Where did we go wrong?

My guess:
We sought to be open minded, to make design processes that would
be more sensitive to life than were the professional practices

of the time. But the result was rigidity: a fixing of aims and
methods to produce designs that everyone now feels to be insensitive to human needs. Another result was that design methods
became more theoretical and many of those drawn to the subject
turned it into the academic study of methods (methodology)
instead of trying to design things better. The language used to
describe designing, and to describe the aims and purposes of
things designed, became more and more abstract. The words lost
touch with how it feels to be a designer and how it feels to
inhabit the systems being designed. Abstract language can often
be a release from the status quo. It was a release in the
beginnings of functionalism, and in the beginnings of design
methods. But it can so easily become fixed, in which case it
turns, overnight, into a tyrrany.
That, I think, is what went wrong. We did not see that what we
proposed was good only as long as it remained a process, and
that it would become bad the moment we allowed it to become a
product. A thing.
And why did the new methods become fixed? Become objects?
My guess, and its only a guess.....

no, I shouldn't say 'only'......the word implies that guessing
is a poor substitute, for 'proof', or for 'logical certainty'
or some such objective statement......but objective statements
are, in the discussion of designing, a delusion, perhaps the
very delusion that set us on the wrong tack?.....they are
'things'...

my guess, my feeling, my impression, my thought about this, is
that, though we saw the need to change the processes of designing we did not see the need to change its aims. We retained the
concept of 'product' as the outcome of designing. We did not
see that we were accepting only a part of the challenge which
we took up : the challenge to transform the idea of progress,
which presumes a specific goal, into the idea of process, which
does not. This transformation is I now realise, a main event
of the twentieth century, though it may have started earlier.
A change which is happening in many areas of life, not only in
design. I'll pause, for a moment, in this most difficult bit

of thinking for me, to name a few examples of the change from
progress to process in other fields of life, before discussing
our blindness over this question of goals.

I've been reading the books of Martin Heidegger, whose way of
doing philosophy can be seen as a change from progress to
process. What he does is to refuse to be drawn into making any
fixed conclusions, concepts, or theories, which are the accepted
aims of Western philosophy. Instead he writes and teaches a mode
of what he calls 'meditative thinking' that is not intended
to reach conclusions but to keep the process of thinking alive.
While this kind of philosophy is happening, while the thinker
is thinking, then its happening. As soon as he reaches a conclusion its over, dead. The aim does not disappear but it
changes its nature. For what Heidegger calls 'calculative thinking', thinking-as-a-means-to-an-end, the aim is external to the
process. The use of thinking to establish truth, certainty; to
control something. But for 'meditative thinking', or what I am
calling process-philosophy, the aim is internal : to maintain
the process. Because, says Heidegger, only while we are
giving our minds to whatever it is that provokes our thoughts
are we being truly human. Calculative thinking being something
that diminishes us, to a degree. His books are full of warnings
that if, through the technologizing of life, calculative thinking
becomes the universal mode of thinking, then the most valuable
part of human life will have gone. That which makes us human.
He does not say that technology and calculative thinking should
be ended but that they must not become the whole of life. He
accepts that, in their way, they are realities, parts of ourselves, something we cannot discard but something we should be
free to accept or refuse according to the occasion.

I've also been drawn to the works of Samuel Taylor Coleridge
who seems, in the early nineteenth century, to foreshadow this
change in the mode of doing philosophy. He repeatedly points
to two meanings of the word 'thought'. It can mean the conclusion, or image, or whatever, that comes to mind. It can
also mean the process of arriving at a conclusion. These two,
he keeps saying, are indivisible : you cannot have one without

the other, just as you cannot have a cake without cooking (though I suppose you can have cooking without cake). His ideas are full of instances of awareness of this relationship between process and its result. The idea of complementarity, as we'd say.

Is there a more practical example than these, of the change from progress to process? What about 'production' itself : the process industries, like chemicals or electricity, or perhaps the construction industry, where the processes are not so obvious? It IS obvious that, in all these cases, there is a continual changing of the nature of the production methods : from making things a few at a time to making them in larger batches or by continuous flow production. The products and their 'consumption patterns' are changing in the same way : from individual arti- facts made 'to last' to disposable goods and service-processes the purpose of which gets harder to explain to unwilling consumers except as a means of creating jobs so that they can earn enough to buy the products and keep the production system going. That is perhaps an unfair description but it does point to a shift of some kind in the relation of means to ends. I'm surprised to see how close is this apparent loss of purpose in industrial production to the 'purposeful purposelessness' which John Cage attempts in his music and which he sees in zen. I remember wondering, at a conference of designers who were trying to come to terms with 'artificial obselescence', (about which they felt guilty) if the throwaway culture IS bad. It's uncannily similar to natural cycles of growth and decay, spring and autumn, birth and death. Our joy and sadness. Consider the lilies. Not only zen, and christianity, but all the religions, seem to have taken up this point as central. They all seem to recommend a giving-up of intentionality, purpose......a giving of oneself. One of the nicest statements I've seen of this is by Rabindranath Tagore, speaking, in his 'song offering' Gitanjali, of the ideas of Indian religion:

> Children have their play on the seashore of worlds. They know not how to swim, they know not how to cast nets. Pearl divers dive for pearls, merchants sail in their ships, while children gather pebbles and scatter them again. They seek not for hidden treasures, they know not how to cast nets.

I'm getting the feeling that this bit of learning that I'm trying
to do is going to reveal that there is nothing to learn. That we
know it already : what was wrong with our methods, or with how
we used them, or failed to. That what we were trying to achieve,
to impose, would happen of its own accord, if only we stopped
trying to make it happen? But I cannot make that jump. I have
to procede, with the process, the process of thinking through
the idea of design-without-product, design as process-in-itself.

I once heard the Italian architect Sergio Los talking of the
using and inhabiting of a building as a process, a physical
process, differing only in scale from the physical process
of constructing the building. In both processes materials and
people move about over the site changing the positions and the
forms of what is there. So, in this view, building is a form
of living and living is a form of building. That's one way of
realising that there are no products, no fixities, only continuous flux. And that designing, making, and using are all processes that are added to, and interact with, the natural processes of the places where these activities occur.

But to return, as I promised, from these examples to my guess
that the new methods became rigid, though they were not intended
to, because we, the method-makers, did not realise that we were
recommending only a part, and not the whole, of the historic
shift from the idea of progress to the idea of process. What we
failed to see, or, if we saw it, what we failed to act on, was
that, though progress has a purpose external to itself, process
does not.

When you go to process, you lose the goal, you lose the aim.

I'm beginning to see it now.......THERE ARE TWO KINDS OF PURPOSES
........the purpose of having a result, something which exists
after the process has stopped, and does not exist until it has
stopped......and there is the purpose of carrying on, of keeping
the process going, just as one may breathe so as to continue
breathing?.......the purpose is to carry on.

In the old idea, the purpose was to STOP, to reach the PROMISED
LAND, the end of progress.......that's it, I think I've grasped
it.

So the fault in method-making was that we made methods as
'products' and handed them on to the designers expecting them
to use them, as 'tools', as means to an end. Which became a
logical trap, turning the idea of process into its opposite?
And many designers rejected these tools, which was fortunate,
perhaps.

We didn't realise that the design-as-process outcome is the
design process....... for everyone.......not for designers...
....we didn't liberate ourselves from being designers.....
designers of predicted outcomes......we didn't drop the role.....

.....we didn't realise that the people inhabiting the world-
designed, if we changed to process-design, have to be designers,
every one of them.....

SUDDENLY MY THINKING SPEEDED UP.....SHOT AHEAD OF TYPING....AHEAD
OF BEING BAFFLED, STUCK....SUDDENLY I CAN SEE AGAIN.......I'LL
try to give the feeling of it in these scraps off the tape I
made when I felt I could not continue the slow, slow, thinking-
and-typing which I've been doing up to now......

          .....they have to be all designers, all designing, all
process, all continuing, never stopping, blah blah blah.....this
is IT!
this is it I'm SURE!....this is, this is, is......terribly roughly
.....this the EDGE, to get over, the phase difference, or
something, the paradigm change, callitwhatyouwill, change of
phase,.....

.....here we are.....designing, now, DOESN'T HAVE AN OUTCOME.....
we were too embarassed to go on with that thought.....we should
have stuck with it.....

.....design has an outcome, a continuation,.....the outcome is

that it continues....and the professionals have to stop being
there AT ALL, in THAT role.....they have to just be people, like
everybody else.....

So it was our talking about design from the point of view of
the professional that made it impossible to GET ON......that
led to that uneasy feeling that the whole business was going
wrong.......

.......talking about design processes in the way we really BEGAN
(with the Indian Village*,and all those other fine thoughts, and
they WERE fine, far finer than what's been thought since) from
the point of view of trying to respond to the interconnectedness
of everything,....if we'd stuck WITH that......(and now we can
still DO that, I think).....if we stick with that idea, if we
HOLD it......the process should go right...?

Chris Alexander, where are you? *

Time for music. The violas. The finale even. No. Not music.
None of that rushing on and on. Its a question of being. Of
being here.

REFERENCES & NOTES

* ALEXANDER. Christopher Alexander's book Notes on the Synthesis of Form, (Harvard University Press, Cambridge, Mass, 1964) & his Indian Village design, were a recurrent topic at the Portsmouth Conference, though he was not present in person.

BROADBENT & WARD. The Portsmouth Conference was organised by Geoffrey Broadbent and Anthony Ward who also edited the proceedings as Design Methods in Architecture (Lund Humphries, London, 1969).

CAGE. I cannot find the several places in his writings where John Cage refers to 'purposeful purposelessness' but the idea permeates most of what he has written about music and life eg in his first book Silence (Wesleyan University Press, Middletown, Conn., 1961).

COLERIDGE. Samuel Taylor Coleridge's ideas are not easy to find and understand and many commentators do not seem to have grasped the point to which I refer, which I found most readily in Owen Barfield's book What Coleridge Thought (Oxford University Press, London, 1971). This book is an attempt to reconstruct, from his scattered writings, the main ideas of the great book of philosophy which Coleridge promised but did not write.

HEIDEGGER. All his writings embody his way of making philosophy a process of thinking rather than its conclusions. Particularly relevant to design and technology are the essays What Calls for Thinking? and The Question Concerning Technology in Martin Heidegger, Basic Writings, edited by David Farrell Krell (Routledge & Kegan Paul, London, 1978).

MILLER. The quotations between horizontal lines (which appear as integral parts of the poem) are from David Miller's poem The Story (Arc Publications, 3&4 Oldroyd, Todmorden, Lancs, Britain, 1976). In case of difficulty finding this, or other, of his writings (they exist only in small

press editions and are often out of print) write to
David Miller, 36 Colville Terrace, London W11.

NICHOLS. W H E Nichols in his as yet uncompleted thesis on
Design Methods, at the Dept of Design, North East London
Polytechnic.

P'EI TI. The verse quoted is from The Pavilion of the Lake,
a section of the Poems of the River Wang by Wang Wei and
P'ei Ti which appears, translated by C J Cohen and Michael
Bullock, in Anthology of Chinese Literature, from Early
Times to the Fourteenth Century, edited by Cyril Birch
(Grove Press, New York, 1965).

TAGORE. The quotation is from Gitanjali (Song Offerings) by
Rabindranath Tagore (originally published in the poet's
own translation from Bengali by Macmillan & Co, London,
1913, and republished extensively).

Looking now at this list of largely poetic quotations, which
enabled me to feel that I was coming close to what is missing
from design as we've known it so far, I am reminded that the
question 'what is it for?' is irrelevant to poetry, as it is
to a tree, or to life itself. Since completing this article
I have been using the names pure design, and contextual design,
to describe this notion of design without purpose, other than
that of fitting what is, which includes both physical nature
and the minds/bodies of all who are involved in the activity
and what it brings into being.

I am reminded also that, for poetry as for life, the role of
objective critic, of outsider, is a dead one, destructive of
what is being created : a new experience. In this new
conception of design, which seems slowly to be appearing here
and there, there is no outside; we are all players. 'We will
play the finale, opus one, number two'......

```
you & I, we, already exist
in this work.  it has no doors.
we already exist in it.
```

"...in the dimension of Time."

This was written for the architecture-and-environment journal
Espacios CEPA, published in Argentina by Ruben Pesci. Ruben
asked for exactly 17 pages to fit a space in a forthcoming
issue (that was the length of another essay which I had promised him but which had to be withdrawn as I'd forgotten it was
already promised to Marina Waisman's journal Summarios). As
there was very little time left to write it in, and as I had
no topic in mind, I used again the method of composing 'camera
ready' on 'prepared pages' bearing quotations chosen and positioned by chance, letting the quotations decide what I was to
write. It was one of the essays that I most enjoyed writing,
free of anxiety and full of surprises. If I remember rightly,
the title was not decided until somewhere near the end of
writing it. But it was quite difficult to write: all that
diversity and not knowing where it led.

After sending the essay off to Argentina I was disappointed to
find that it was not going to be published after all as the
journal was re-organised, and is now called Ambiente. However,
on a later visit to Argentina I met Ruben and he promised to
print it eventually in the new journal, together with an interview. An edited and typset version of the english text first
appeared in Design Studies, volume 1, number 3, in January 1980.
I am grateful to Butterworth Scientific Ltd (PO Box 63, Westbury
House, Bury Street, Guildford, Surrey, GU2 5BH) for permission
to reproduce it here.

This text is reproduced from the original typescript.

Looking for a way to begin this article I came across the last
paragraph of Marcel Proust's Remembrance of Things Past in
which he realises that each of us exists, outside the dimension
of space, as an immense (perhaps grotesque) being,"plunged
into the years",consisting, at any moment, of the effects and
memories of all that we have experienced in our lives.   What
becomes of design if we try to make it operate in time as well
as in space? And if we accept that each person is a lifetime?

> Bruce asked me to advise him about a chair he was
> designing. I realized in talking with him that its
> probably a mistake to impose one's ideas upon a product,
> an object. Better to use one's design ability to design
> a process by which the object can be shaped by the users
> and by the whole situation.

That quotation, like the others which I have already chosen
for this article, was picked by a chance process from the
books and papers about me as I write here, in London, and,
like the other quotations, has been pre-typed on the page
at a position which has also been picked by chance. Thus,
in composing the article, I am faced with a task that is
in some ways similar to that of a designer who has decided
to make his design process, and the resulting design, sensitive
not only to his present ideas but to his past, and to the
past activities and lives of others. A deliberate attempt
to compose something not so much by conscious intention
and control, but by letting what already exists arouse the
ideas that are being given form and substance here.

In the case of Bruce's chair I was appalled, as always[*],by
the high degree to which his designs and sketches imposed,
upon the wood and other materials he intended to use, a
conception of 'what is a chair' and 'what is sitting' that
owed much to all the designs seen in glossy magazines and
very little to the exact nature of materials, of production
processes, and of the very varied ways in which people
actually sit. Nearly every design one sees, it seems to me,

[*] not only by this design, but by most designs

is so strong a reflection of our ignorance of the lives of
those for whom its intended and of the designer's assumption
that his thinking is adequate to what he is doing to the
world. Poor world. What are we doing to it?

But, as soon as I catch myself typing that deadly word 'it',
I realise that the world is not an it, is not a thing, detached
from ourselves. It is ourselves. The world is not just the
earth and sea and sky and plants and animals and houses and
roads and cities and cars and farms etc. It is also our lives,
our experiences and memories, our minds. When we say 'the
world', and when we call it an 'it', we are making a false
distinction between the things we perceive and the
processes of perception and recognition by which we learn to
see and act. It is obvious, as soon as one stops to think
about it, that an abstract word like 'world' is not the name
of an object. It is the name of a great mass of shared
experience out of which we infer the existence of the planet
earth and of all the things upon it. For everyday living
it is of course necessary and appropriate to use this verbal
convention as if it were a fact, but when we are designing,
when we are trying make a change, or an improvement to what
we call world, it is surely right and necessary to understand what it is we are really doing, and not base our
decisions on words that we know to contain a false picture
of reality. Designing, as I see it now, is, or could be, the
process of unlearning what we know of what exists, of what we
call the 'status quo', to the point where we are able to lose
our pre-conceptions sufficiently to understand the life, and
lives, for which we design,   and where we are aware of
the ways in which new things, added to the world, can change
the way we see it. Visiting a foreign country, or returning
after many years to a place one knew, one feels immediately
the surprise of a person whose ideas have ceased to fit reality.

Any probing of perception seems to quickly undo so many
assumptions. And to dispose immediately of the mind-
body split. I'm amazed that so far perception theory
seems not to have dented both physics and philosophy,

making nonsense of the humanist position. There is no
human. There is no life. Let alone "other planets".
These are words. Are words these?. What is. This
degree of uncertainty, that's good, surely, and real.
No need to fear the universe. Or to DEPEND on words.
Deepend. The words are real words. Absolutely! But
really nothing else. Yet we do communicate, we think we
do. The sender usually. But communication's probably
in fact the other way round, an opening of oneself to
others to perceive more than we think? Here too? What
will others see through this that's hidden from me now?

I wrote that in 1976, while composing a book of memories of
what I'd been writing and thinking over twenty-five years:
writings remembered. Why is it that so much of what has been
learnt of reality, and of how we perceive it, how we ARE
what we perceive, has so far had little or no effect upon
how we organise life? Why are we ignoring the main discoveries of our time, in art and science (eg relativity,
the uncertainty principle, the findings of Cezanne) in our
attempts to understand and solve the massive problems of
the twentieth century, problems arising from our own inter-
ventions in the world of nature and of mind? When I ask such
a question I can feel myself getting angry, impatient at the
seemingly too-slow evolution of the processes of planning and
design to cope with the situation brought about by these very
processes. But then I ask myself if I am right. Ideas, however right they may be, can be realised only at the pace of
life and experience of those to whom they refer. And through
the seemingly imperfect understandings of each of us, our
minds, our ways of organising experience, being so amazingly
different from one person to the next. Perhaps its a wonder
that things go as well as they do? These are new thoughts
for me. In the past I've felt a moral duty to try to apply,
or even to impose, what I conceive as being the right way
of doing things. But now, after some years outside the worlds
of practice and designing, and while interesting myself in
what I call the time arts (music, film, theatre, poetry etc)

,and in oriental thinking, I am beginning to be more willing
to accept the pace of evolution and not to try to force it.
I can see, very readily, from my experience with design methods,
that, when one attempts to introduce a new idea of how something
should be done, that its either ignored, as design methods were
in the fifties, or, worse than that, its misunderstood and
applied in a way that contradicts the original reasons for
seeking a new method. In the case of design methods my
intention was to find ways to make the design process more
sensitive to life but what happened was the imposition of
methods that were of a larger scale than those we had before
but which are less sensitive. Rationality, originally seen
as the means to open up the intuition to aspects of life
outside the designer's experience, became, almost overnight,
a toolkit of rigid methods that obliged designers and planners
to act like machines, deaf to every human cry and incapable
of laughter. That's what made me leave designing, for a
while at least. And, once I'd left it, I found that the
first person from whom I tried to learn, in the world of
music, John Cage, was engaged in a vast essay on world
improvement, which he titled "Diary: How To Improve The
World (You Will Only Make Matters Worse)". The Cagean method
of composing not only music but life itself was, I learnt, to
give up intention, to seek unpredictable results. Indeterminacy.
In place of control. Accepting what we did not choose.

> I think that the systems approach is inherently ambiguous,
> it isn't entirely objective,
> that it does involve a drastic shift
> from mechanical thinking,
> with fixed aims,
> and one-track processes,
> like railway lines from A to B.
> Systems thinking, quite obviously,
> is a way of looking at all the things that are
> connected with each other,
> and everything is in the end,
> ......but certainly looking at the
> more obvious connections between things.

This, as those writing about it often say,
is mainly an attitude, a state of mind.
......If you have the systems attitude
you will immediately feel the sense
of trying out complex systems, (eg transport, education, etc)
several at a time,
to discover their interactions.
In an experimental city......
If you are not normally a systems-thinking person,
you wont feel this as an instantly acceptable idea.
It will be a puzzling idea,
you'll think 'how expensive' 'what's the point?'.

Interviewer:
This idea of the systems approach
is very different from what is sometimes called
the systems approach,
that's things like systems engineering,
and operations research....

Yes, that's the number-crunching,
input-output analysis approach,
where you do look at the interactions,
but only within systems that are pre-specified,
....like designing a chemical plant
where only the choice of existing components,
and the pattern of the pipes,
is the main decision.

That's taken from a tape-recorded interview in which I was
being asked, by Robin Roy, to explain some ideas about experimental cities and to justify my confidence (in 1972) in
the systems approach. I am amazed now, in listening to it
for the first time since the interview, that I was at the
time unaware that the popular use of this term refers to
a rigid kind of system approach that is practically the
opposite of what I had in mind and what I'd learnt from
such pioneers of the idea as Norbert Weiner, West Churchman,
and others. Somehow the inspiring aspect of seeing-the-

world as an interacting system was replaced, as soon as the
idea reached practical application, by the deadening notion
of representing the whole of life by a rational block-
diagram which is limited to those aspects of life that are
capable of measurement and of calculation. Which, of course,
(though we did not see it at the time) excludes much, or all,
of what makes life worth living. That which is incalculabe.
That which cannot be put into words, unless they are used
poetically, with real feeling........I remember some words
of Fredrico Garcia Lorca which Cristina Caffaro read at my
lecture in Rosario to remind us of this. They are from the
prologue to his comedy The Shoemaker's Prodigious Wife:

> THE AUTHOR: Worthy spectators.......The poet does not
> ask benevolence, but attention, since long ago he leapt
> that barbed fence of fear that authors have of the
> theatre. Because of this absurd fear, and because the
> theatre on many occasions is run for financial reasons,
> poetry retires fron the stage in search of other surr-
> oundings where people will not be shocked at the fact
> that a tree, for example, should become a puff of smoke,
> or that three fishes through their love for a hand should
> be changed into three million fishes to feed the hunger
> of a multitude. The author has preferred to set the
> dramatic example in the live rhythm of an ordinary little
> shoemaker's wife. Everywhere walks and breathes the
> poetic creature that the author has dressed as a shoe-
> maker's wife with the air of a refrain or a simple
> ballad, and the audience should not be surprised if she
> appears violent or takes bitter attitudes because she
> is ever fighting, fighting with the reality which encircles
> her and with fantasy when it becomes visible reality.
>   (Shouts of THE SHOEMAKER'S WIFE are heard: I want to
>   come out!)
> I'm hurrying! Don't be so impatient to come out; You're
> not going to wear a dress with a long train and matchless
> plumes; but a torn dress; do you hear? The dress of the
> shoemaker's wife.

(Voice of THE SHOEMAKER'S WIFE is heard: I want to come
out!)
Silence!
(The curtain is drawn and the darkened stage appears.)
Every day in the cities it dawns like this, and the audience
forgets its half-world of dreams to go to market just as
you enter your house, prodigious little shoemaker's wife.
(The light is increasing.)
Let's start! You come in from the street.
(Voices and arguing are heard. To the audience.)
Good evening.
(He takes off his tall silk hat and it becomes illuminated
with a green light from within. The AUTHOR tips it over and
a gush of water falls from it. The AUTHOR looks at the
audience a bit embarrassedly, and retires backward, with
great irony.)
I beg your pardon. (Exit.)

That quotation's an exception: it was not chosen in advance,
by chance, but deliberately, now. It reminds me of a perfect
evening when chance processes had seemingly magical harmony
with the life of Rosario. Discussing silence, as the most
extreme example of uncomposed music, I paused, for a full
minute, before continuing to speak. Almost as soon as I
stopped talking the clock struck eight. And later, when I
demonstrated John Cage's piece of music, which consists of
four minutes thirty-three seconds of silence, a bat flew in
at one window and out at another. And there was the lecture
in Buenos Aires when I went into the street to get cool before
beginning, only to get drenched by a bucket of water thrown
from an upper window! The more I abandon cautious planning
in favour of chance, and of acting on slight impulses, the more
I wonder at what I have been missing.

......if we do go in for experimental cities,
of a kind which does not consist of
one lot of people pushing something onto another lot,
but genuineopenness collectiveopenness to the future,

a conversation about the things which could be made to
happen,
if it becomes a kind of physical conversation about the
future,
through people trying things out,
and the political difficulties of doing that
are solved somehow or other,
goodness knows how,
with new kinds of political institutions,
new kinds of legal systems,
more dynamic than those we have,
......if all that comes about, then,
I would expect it to be important
not to start with a collection of experimental cities
which the people now living think are right,
and fit their expectations.
We should expect quite unpromising things,
or even threatening things,
to turn out to be different when we try them.
And quite promising things,
like most of the utopias,
suggested by Plato, and by many other people since,
for which the recipies read well,
but for which, in retrospect,
there is always a hidden fault......

......for argument's sake we might start with half
of the experimental cities of that type,
which <u>look</u> promising,
and half that definitely don't,
and just wait and see what happens.
Unless there's some genuine doubt
its no good investing such effort anyway,
......unless we are really open-minded
as to whether its good or bad,
what's the point of experimenting?

More words from the interview. Robin Roy was questioning me

about an article that I wrote for Design in 1966. It was my
first against designing and it was popular with the young
doubters-of-the-system of the nineteen-sixties. I remember
now that the article was itself a transcription of a radio
talk: here it is now being transcribed once again from tape
to writing. In the original article, and perhaps in the
radio talk too (I've forgotten what I said), I was criticising
existing methods of design, those used by the professions,
as being "conservative, persuasive, and rigid" and I was
suggesting that instead of fixed professional planning
processes we should try a more public way of designing, with
much more doubt and openness. My suggestion was the test-city,
as I called it, in which many new ways of life could be tried
out before everyone is committed to any one of them by large-
scale irreversible investment such as created the new towns
around London. I was thinking of something much less permanent
and more flexible: a site, resembling an airfield, in which,
using all sorts of improvisations and simulations of new types
of buildings, communications, transports, educations, productions,
agricultures, etc, a completely new way of living would be
tried out, probably by volunteers or perhaps by paid adventurers.
The design principle was to test the most unexpected and
unpredictable aspects of new systems : the interactions
between them. And more important than that, to discover the
extent to which, through experience and adaptation, the ideas
of the explorers of these new ways of life, the experimental
anthropologists one might call them, would change. I'd expect,
from some experience of testing new products one-at-a-time,
that initial reactions to the prospect of life in some proposed test city would be no guide at all to opinions of those
who had tried it out.for a year or two. But how, I ask myself
now, would people ever get into the relaxed and confident state
of mind to permit such experiments to take place, at public
expense, and as a replacement of the professional practices
which now control so much of human evolution, under such
names as architecture, engineering, industrial design, planning,
market research, investment policy, and many kinds of legislation? For without some collective equivalent of the gifted

180

and inventive person's mind no such experiment can be expected
to discover anything new. Collective inventiveness, and
intelligence: that seems to be the quality most needed in
design, a quality without which the new design methods are
ineffective. The ability to act upon an intuition, with
suspended judgement. To risk, to enjoy, to learn from, the
finding out of the extent to which one's picture of reality
can change.......that's not something one can do an a
drawing board, or by computer simulations of behaviour. You
have to live it. As the pioneers of alternative technology,
and alternative lifestyles,are beginning to do for themselves
without any encouragement from the rest of us who, one day, may
be thankful for what they are finding out.

> 5 December 1978
> It looks as if the idea of beginning a design by writing
> specifications of the performance requirements needs
> revision so that one can be sensitive, especially at the
> start, to the interdependancy of problem and solution.
> Probably this is the entry-point to 'mind' in designing,
> the bridge to real thought, and away from cumbersome
> design systems and procedures that swamp one, or get
> abandoned.

My note, made at a computer conference, was written in a state
of both encouragement (at the intelligent interest which the
designers and engineers of computer software are showing in
design methods) and alarm (at the rigid way in which the
designing of this most expensive and influential new design-
product is being carried out). I was surprised to discover,
when I recently got a little involved in the designing of
software, that it is far more like craftwork than design-
by-drawing and that software designers, unlike most designers,
can seldom make a fresh start, most of their work being tied
to the adaptation of large pieces of existing software. Under
this circumstance it is hard to see how anyone can get the
room for manoevre that is essential if anything new is to
emerge....how designers and users can recover presence of mind?

A story. Once the environment was considered as
everything outside the body of a human being. The
environment was the place where things happened. A
stone was pushed off a log and it fell and the falling
was a new piece of information that could be compared
to what a stone did when it was still. Slowly it became
interesting to think of all the other things the stone
could do and what this reflected was an awareness of the
doing that human beings were capable of. Then the action
of the stone and the activity of pushing it became laws
and experiments. Later the entire process was made into
a small and comprehensible model and all the states of
the stone that were possible were considered as either
"yes" or "no" states. Then the process of describing
created the thing described although the stone and the
log were still there. Later the model and the description and the stone and the log and the activity of pushing
and the environment disappeared and the people disappeared
and what remained was a dynamic description and series of
events without the divisions and nominal relationships.

The history of science? And a criticism, perhaps, of the
concept of "environment" if it is taken to mean something
that excludes ourselves, our thoughts and action? The words
come from Edwin Schlossberg's letter to Gregory Bateson and
were written for a book about Bateson's work, and particularly
his concept of "an ecology of mind". When I took leave of
design I was reacting against   what I called the
'inhuman' use of abstract functional language to describe and
fix life in the dreary and numbing formulae of design method-
ologists, environmentalists, ecologists, and others. Somehow, I felt, my friends, those with the good intentions of
improving life, had become the enemies of mankind, of ourselves
as persons. Then, at a conference, I met Edwin Schlossberg,
and was amazed to find that, though he seemed to share my
distrust of concepts like 'environment', he was using what
I called 'machine language' (abstract terms) to describe
people. And, when I eventually began to understand something

182

of what he was saying and writing on this topic, I was even
more surprised to discover that he had more or less invented
a way of using words, abstract or concrete, that really
seem to correct the error of mistaking abstractions for
things.....Even now I cannot put into any adequate phrase
the sense I have that he has developed a way of talking and
writing about 'mind', and all lesser entities, which evades
the traps of unreality to which philosophy is prone, and
which, in our world of design, seems to have driven design
methods out of its right place as a practical way of
enlivening design and into the sterile function of being
a vehicle for some pretty useless and fruitless academic
nonsense. That's how I saw it in 1973, when I was driven
to compose the first of what became a series of 'conference
plays' written in protest against the inhumanity of the
language of design conferences. Plays in which characters
like Immanuel Kant speak a far better kind of abstract
thinking than we designers seem to be capable of, and in which
others, like Walt Whitman, speak, as antidote, about their
feelings and of more everyday concerns.

What IS the context of design? I seem to have two answers:
it is our minds, our lives, as persons, as beings able always
to imagine, to perceive, to remember,and to be,beyond the
range of whatever others who may try to serve our needs or
control our behaviour can foretell: it is also 'evolution',
the so slow, and seemingly mindless evolution of all things,
natural and artificial, which so often seems to exclude the
'most rational' or 'most intelligent' actions and to encourage
what looks like sheer stupidity. But again, when we attend
to what exists in an open state of mind, free of intention,
or the will to control, 'evolution', or 'nature' seems the
sweetest thing, the marvel of existence, the source of all
delight? Mind and evolution, each a terror but a joy in unison.

I......became aware how much your writing allows for
evolution in the context of thinking. As you suggest,
what evolves is the context and not the entities.......

This letter evolves because of its relationship to the
writer, to the reader......and so on, and not in and of
itself. Perhaps if I rewrite it some day it will change,
but it will be rewritten because the context in which it
exists has changed and so requires alteration.

More of Edwin's letter to Gregory Bateson. I like so much that
little jolt to my thinking by the notion, new to me, that 'things'
do not evolve but context does. Is evolution, then, the process
of seeking to re-establish harmonies with context, a context that
spontaneously changes? And is design this same seeking, or should
it be? Intention, in designing, according to this view of things,
would then be appropriate only as the means to get to the state
of accord with context, the state of harmony, bliss perhaps,
which intention destroys?....Is designing, then, a dangerous
weapon to be used only when things have got into a mess, and
something to be avoided when life is going well? The context of
design, according to this apparent reversal of the usual view
of it as positive, is 'problem', life gone wrong. And, in
particular, the splitting of mind from matter, persons from
nature. The underlying problem of modern times? In this light,
'bad' design is that which perpetuates this fundamental split,
or alienation, between each of us,as persons,and 'the world',
as we so destructively describe our situation. And 'good'
design is that which tends to heal the split, and, in doing
so, to make designing unnecessary........achieves a state
which intentionality would destroy?

I did not expect my simple question "what becomes of design if
we try to make it operate in time?" lead me so far. At last I
feel I am understanding some of the impulses which led me to
retire from design and to busy myself with the seemingly
useless activities of musicians, poets, artists and philosophers.......But the variety of these thoughts, arising from
the decision to let this article be guided by some chance
quotations, seems, for the moment, too much for me. As a
reader, of the writing, I am getting lost. Time to go to bed.

Next day:
I awoke disturbed, but soon, making some notes of what was in

my mind, I found my thoughts returning to the quotation from
my notes at the computer conference, and to the idea that to
begin a design by writing specifications of 'what's needed' is
to close one's mind, to lose the room for manoeuvre that you
must have if you are to discover anything new. Computer software designers, if they are tied to the adaptation of existing
designs, may well find clear specifications a real help in
trying to design in muddled situations. But obviously they
lack, at present, the freedom to rethink the whole idea of
'why are we using computers anyway?' or 'what are we doing to
life?'. My thoughts this morning let me see that, as with the
term 'system design', I have been in the habit of using the
technical language of design in a far wider sense than is
commonly meant. I remember now that I have often advocated a
version of 'specification writing' that is not at the scale of
'needs' as felt by existing users, who are adapted to the status
quo, but at the scale of 'why are we doing it anyway?', the scale
of what today I'd call creative disturbance: the letting-go, of
our immediate self-interests, that reveals our larger selves.

> Arriving at Austin (we were met at the airport with gifts
> of Texas wild flowers) I visited the city dumps and found
> they were hardly suitable for a conference. There is no
> rubbish to be seen, only bulldozers moving the earth to
> cover everything as soon as it arrives. Then we found
> a more romantic dump, such as I must have had in mind,
> one in which unwanted objects are just left alone under
> the trees. But the owner of this dump would not let us
> meet there as he is being criticised for having it. I
> was about to give up when I realised why it is that I like
> dumps so much and the reasons why I'd felt them related
> to the conference theme: the theme of applying the
> principles of living organisms to dead buildings. I
> realised that what I like about dumps is that they consist
> of man-made things released from the bondage of purpose,
> that, once in the dump, the things have no function, they've
> lost their names. We are free to use them in new ways,
> or to ignore them, as we are with natural objects.

My contribution, to that conference on 'environmental evolution',
was the suggestion that we try to hold it on a dump, where we
would be obliged to survive, to improvise shelters etc, for
the three days of the conference. As nobody wanted to join
me in this I had to start on my own looking for a dump where
I could live out the suggestion and see what happened. In the
end, not finding the kind of dump I'd imagined, I stayed under
an oak tree in the carpark outside the conference hall,
arguing that a carpark is a temporary dump consisting of
abandoned mobile architecture. Eventually several people joined
me and some nice experiences ensued. They were some of the
pleasantest days of my life. People brought me food, and a
sleeping bag, and someone lent me a van to sleep in. And the
organisers of the conference said, afterwards, that it turned
out to be a nice extension of the conference as most people
came out to the park where we had informal discussions and
made some experiments in experiencing the friendliness, or the
unfriendliness, of our reception when we visited nearby
buildings. The results of these experiments went against our
expectations, the big brutal-looking tower block being far
friendlier than the small human-looking building, and the
empty house we entered allowing a sense of freedom that one
can almost never get indoors. A building, I realise now, is
not just the material its made of, however beautiful that may
be, or however 'well-designed', but the complete ensemble of
building/people/their roles/the life being led inside it. And,
as with objects on a dump, the empty building, nobody's territory, has a quality, shared with beaches, forests, and the like,
that is very pleasant but is excluded from 'man-made-world' by
our insistence that everything shall 'have a purpose'. Bad
design includes, in this view of it, bad using of things, mis-
using of 'world', of what is given, by nature, by each other.

So what becomes of the idea that design is negative, a response
to world gone wrong, misused, that designing is a disturbance,
an opening of the door to chaos, creative chaos? In my note
this morning I realised a reason why, perhaps, so many of
what seemed to me to be constructive design proposals are
rejected. It is that, in asking such broad questions as 'why

are we doing it anyway?' the person trying to apply the new
design methods in the spirit in which they were meant to be
used is threatening not only the existence of 'cars', 'schools',
'computers' or whatever, but is threatening the social relations,
such as those of family, or job, on which most people depend.
The destructive element in this approach to design is that it does
not acknowledge the right to stability in one's relationships.
But is there such a right? A right to hold everyone down to
the status quo so that you and I can continue, indefinitely,
our being,just as it is, together? Edwin Schlossberg, in his
book How I Learn How I Learn wrote

> I do not understand why the woods do not have walls.
> The section of the words that is most interesting is that
> part which sets you to some incredible flight of wonder.
> I am seriously (now you know) concerned with the act of
> posture which disallows growth. Like twisting to assume
> invisibility or familiar shape.

'I am responsible for you', 'I only work here'......are these
the postures he is thinking of......? Postures which recognise
that others exist, or that 'I' exist, at the reduced scale of
role but not, I feel, at the proper scale, the immense scale, of
'person'. The scale of 'mind', the largest scale of all, outside
the reach of all calculation, all measurement. The scale most
easily to be felt in myth, in dream, in fantasy, in fiction.
But everything IS fiction. That's just the point with which
these words began, the acknowledging that there is no stable
world, apart from the words we use to make it seem to be a thing,
a fixity, a fact. Human life, it seems, has, so far, been
organised around a diminished, and false, view of the size of
a person. And of our need, if we are to develop, to grow, to
really 'be', to change. Our constant need to keep changing
if we are to be free to adjust ourselves to 'context', to
'world', to 'reality', to unite mind with body, with all variety.

> ......I should not fail, even if the result were to make
> them resemble monsters, to describe men first and foremost
> as occupying a place, a very considerable place compared

with the restricted one which is allotted to them in space,
a place on the contrary immoderately prolonged - for simultaneously, like giants plunged into the years, they touch
epochs that are immensely far apart, separated by the slow
accretion of many, many days - in the dimension of Time.

The last words of Marcel Proustb last book Time Regained. Having
been inspired to begin with the last five of these words I chose
to end with their context, and to let chance decide their
position on the last of my pieces of paper. Which leaves me a
little space to think how this vast, compassionate, but perhaps
unedifying picture of 'a person' being the accumulating total
of his or her memories of life, relation, action, good or bad,
may disturb the peace I keep seeking, I think, in these thoughts
of extending the dimensions of design from those of space to
that of time. Not that I think time is in any way a 'dimension',
a line, a track of 'progress'. That whole idea seems wrong.
Time, I'll say for want of any worthwhile definition, is, as
Proust describes it (not as he names it in this comparison
with lines in space):'simultaneously, like giants plunged into
the years, they touch epochs......far apart'. 'It', 'life',
is, among other things, a process, not a progress, and so is
design, or it should be, can be. A process of re-membering,
re-making oneself, constantly, out of all one's past, one's
world, a world in which I am the contents of the worlds of
others, as they are of mine......?

But this is all so serious. And perhaps, like Proust's picture
of life, my view is coloured more by having lived than by
waiting to begin, without regrets......
What about the blonde who caught my eye, in that advertisement,
she was adjusting her bra, those two people, coming out of door
into the street, or the woman in blue, running after them, the
two children, leaning against the railings......

dear Mr Jones
During the past three decades there has been a growing concern
about the progress of technology and the......

SOURCES

The sources of the quotations are:

"Bruce asked..." is from <u>Dear Architects and Others Who Imagine</u>
<u>How</u> a book I've written and published myself (Jones Family
Editions, London, 1975).

"Any probing..." is from <u>Writings Remembered</u>, another book
written and published by myself, as above, in 1976.

"I think..." is from the audio cassette <u>Aspects of Systems</u>
<u>Designing</u> prepared by Robin Roy for the Open University,
Milton Keynes, Britain (Side 2, Unit 32-34, T100 AC7), 1972.

* "THE AUTHOR:..." is from the prologue to the play The
Shoemaker's Prodigious Wife in <u>Five Plays, Comedies and</u>
<u>Tragicomedies</u> by Federico Garcia Lorca, translated by James
Graham-Lujan and Richard L O'Connell, Secker & Warburg, 1965
and Penguin Books, Harmondsworth, 1970.

"......if we do go" is from Robin Roy's tape cassette, as
above.

"5 December" is from my notes.

"A story" is from Edwin Schlossberg's letter For My Father
in <u>About Bateson</u> edited by John Brockman, E P Dutton, New York,
1977.

"I......became" is also from Edwin Schlossberg's letter, as
above.

"Arriving at" is from <u>Dear Architects</u>, as above.

"I do not..." is from the book <u>How I Learn How I Learn</u> written
and published by Edwin Schlossberg, Chester, Massachusetts, 1977.

continuous design and
redesign

This was written at the invitation of Les Belady of IBM who
was organising a conference on long-life software (that is
computer software which is re-used and modified so that it
can match new generations of hardware and new situations and
systems). The paper was reproduced in the pre-conference
book Long-Life Software, The Sixty-Seventh Infotech State-
of-the-Art Conference, London, 10-12 December 1979, Infotech
International Limited, Maidenhead, Berkshire but the proceedings were not published subsequently. An edited and
typeset version of the paper appeared in Design Studies,
volume 4, number 1, in January 1983.

As this is another essay that was written camera-ready on
prepared pages the original typescript is reproduced here as
that is the form in which it was composed and is intended to
be read: as a trace, or record, of a process of thinking and
writing.

PART ONE   What can be learnt from other fields?

In planning this part of the paper I have chosen eight kinds
of evolution or designing from which I am hoping to learn
something that may be relevant to the special problems of
continuous design, & re-design, that occur in the making,
and remaking, of computer software. (I say 'making', not
designing, because a programmer, unlike a designer in other
fields, is himself both designer-and-maker; the medium of
design is not a symbolic model of the product, it is the
product itself.)

In preparation for thinking how these eight kinds of
planned or unplanned change may relate to the process of
changing, modifying, maintaining, updating, large software
systems I have limited myself to one or two examples of
each and to a page of comment. The examples have been pre-
positioned on each page, leaving me to find words, fitting
both my thoughts and the spaces left between the page-titles
and the examples. Thus, my process for writing the paper
resembles, to an extent, the process of re-thinking and
re-designing within the limits of something that already
exists, turning what might seem to be constraints into
sources of inspiration.

Continuous design and re-design is a concept new to me. My
previous thinking and experience has always been of design as
'the initiation of change, or newness, in man-made things'.
So I have very little idea of how this rethinking, from a
seemingly very different conception of design,is going to
turn out.

NATURAL EVOLUTION

The term 'survival of the fittest' is not of much help in
trying to understand how natural evolution occurs. Its not
the organism that evolves, its the context. When a change
in the environment decreases the chances of survival of the
normal, or 'fittest', members of a population,some of the
more freakish, or 'unfit', members may find they can survive
better than they did. Thus, in response to evolution of
context, the freaks become the norm and many of the 'fit'
have fewer descendants, who thus become rarer, more freakish.

> ......a classic case of evolution has been the appearance
> over the last hundred years of black ('melanic') moths in
> areas where the vegetation is blackened by industrial
> pollution. It has happened independently in England,
> Germany, and Japan...... (J Z Young.)

This process, the slow adjustment of living activities of
populations to meet varying conditions, as J Z Young called
it, is completely different from the conscious deliberate
planning and designing that we are used to in the evolution of
the man-made. There is no conscious plan, no teleology,
no sense of purpose, no way in which an individual can itself
evolve. Change is accidental, occurring between, not within,
generations. Yet it has such subtle and 'well organised' results.

What, if anything, can we learn, from this form of continuous
change in the shapes of incredibly complex organisms? 'Watch
the context' seems to me to be the lesson, the common ground
between the otherwise incomparably different processes of
natural selection and intentional design. Paying attention
to changes in conditions, and being in readiness to respond
to them, may not be as easy as it sounds when one is perceiving
the world through eyes that have become adapted to seeing only
what fits one's aims and objectives, which may themselves be
a function of the kind of design one is paid to think about.
The irrelevance of a change to the way one is designing now
may signal its relevance to how one ought to be designing.

ADAPTATION OF ORGANISMS

Each of these elderberry leaves, though of recognisably the
same 'design', is different in both shape and size. The large
leaf is seemingly 'malformed' along one edge and each leaf was,
before I cut the stem and flattened the leaves for xeroxing,
curved differently in three dimensions, probably to reach the
light. This variation of one design to fit differing conditions
is even more evident in animals than it is in plants. A sparrow,
such as the one which came near as I was planning this paper,
changes the whole of its shape, moment to moment, redesigning
itself by its power to move about and to twist, turn, swell,
shrink, according to its sensing of what's all around it, food,
threat, or whatever. Not to mention flying. How, I asked
myself, are organisms able to adapt individually, and so variously,
to differing circumstances while retaining, so precisely, the
form they share with others of the same species?

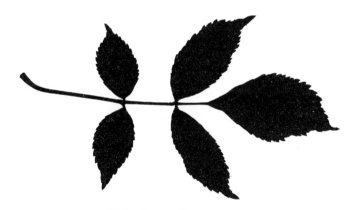

Elderberry leaves

I arrived at what is perhaps a partial answer by noticing that
the sparrow changed its size quite drastically, every second or
so, by moving its feathers outward or inward all over its body.
Each sub-unit of all of its apparently homogeneous surface being,
I guessed, free to react independently to external conditions
such as cold, or threatening movement. The adaptive units are
at a different scale from that of the organism, the design.

Owen Barfield, writing about poetic language, gives this example:

> Thlee-piecee bamboo, two-piecee puff-puff, walk-along
> inside, no-can-see.

It is Pidgin English for a three-masted steamship with two
funnels. This foreign, and original, choice of words enables
us, though familiar with both dictionary-english and the normal
view of steamships, to "shed....civilization like an old garment",
as Barfield puts it, and see the world, for a moment, through
experience very different from our own. Is this a bizarre
example of the normal process through which languages evolve:
through the re-using of words, in almost total disregard for
previous meanings, to name experiences and phenomena previously
nameless? Barfield notes that Shakespeare was the probable
author of the modern meaning of several of the key-terms in
the abstract thinking of our time. 'Function' is one:

> Dark night, that from the eye his function takes
> (Shakespeare, 1590)

> Let us take a function a little more complicated, $u=ax^2$
> (Babbage, 1779)

Two examples taken from the history of the word in the Oxford
Dictionary. Before 1590 the word apparently meant only the
function, role, activity, of a person or class, eg ruling : the
function of a king. Shakespeare is noted as the first to
write of a bodily organ in this way. Is that like calling a
mast a bamboo? Every abstract term, Barfield implies,is
'petrified metaphor' deriving originally from description of
natural events. The logician, he says, is obliged, to obtain
obedience to his arbitrary 'laws' of thought, to reduce
meanings of words to as near zero as possible. But the growth
of language appears to disregard dictionary meanings and to
use words according to accidental similarities outside those
meanings. Why, in language, is this disobedience creative,
not confusing; why are dictionaries so dead?

CRAFT EVOLUTION

The more I see of software designing the more I notice resemblance
not to design in other fields but to craftsmanship. In each the
designing, if such it can be called, is done by the maker, and
there is much fitting, adjusting, adapting of existing designs,
and much collaboration, with little chance of a bird's eye
view, such as the drawing board affords, of how the whole thing
is organised, though, in craft evolution, if not in software,
the results have the appearance of natural organisms or of
exceptionally well integrated designs. But there is an important difference: software is increasingly made by modifying the
actual material of previous pieces of software, as a building
may be altered for a new use, whereas a waggon-maker, for
instance, modifies the form, but does not re-use the material,
in making each small step in the gradual evolution of his
product. As in natural evolution, each alteration is made
without conscious intention, or plan, of what kind of artifact
may later appear out of the seemingly blind process of making
corrections, here and there, as and when lack of adaptation
to the working conditions, or to the materials or the making
process, become evident. But there is a tremendous respect
for the form, as it has evolved so far, embodying, as it does,
the otherwise unrecorded history of a thousand ways in which
the artifact and its context can be attuned. Of course the
context has to be stable, within limits, for centuries, for
craft evolution to be possible. Is there any way, I ask
myself, in trying to learn from these various modes of evolution,
for the makers of software, and the users of it, to attain this
almost magical accord with context when context is itself in flux?

......farm-waggons had been adapted, through ages, so very
closely to their own environment that, to understanding
eyes, they really looked almost like living organisms.
They were so exact. Just as a biologist may see, in any
limpet, signs of the rocky shore, the smashing breakers,
so any provincial wheelwright could hardly help reading,
from the waggon-lines, tales of haymaking and upland fields,
of hilly roads and noble horses, and so on. (George Sturt.)

NEW VERSIONS OF EXISTING DESIGNS

My experience of designing began with industrial design, which,
in the fifties, was a new design profession devoted to the re-
thinking and re-shaping of existing designs of manufactured
products. The typical design process was for a design consultant,
(who did not work for one industry, but several, and was trained
in art not engineering) to be given a brief to re-design the
appearance,and to re-think how it is used, while retaining, to
varying degrees, the existing interior mechanisms and the
existing manufacturing plant. Although meeting much resistance,
at first, from engineering designers, salesmen, and others,
whose experience was limited to making and selling the existing
design, the technique prevailed and now many manufactured
products are designed this way by people of wider training and
outlook than that of an industry geared to one type of product.
Quite a revolution. What, in essence, was the process of this
kind of re-designing? At its worst it was cosmetics, restyling,
the imposition, via the introduction of an operationally separated
cover-component, of a fashionable appearance calculated to increase
sales while minimising costly disruption of the expensive tooling-
up of the mechanical parts, which were hidden from view. Top-
down designing, aided by a physical separation from the engineering,
which had been designed bottom-up. At its best industrial design
means the deriving of a fresh concept for the product as a whole
from a radical appraisal of the relevance of both inner and outer
components and of the operations of using it (now called ergonomics)
so as to find a design that is noticeable better from every point
of view. In this re-thinking stability is discarded, at the physical
scale,and re-created at the scale of functions, costs, sales.

    stretched versions of a passenger jet
    successive revised editions of a popular textbook

In many cases these are less deliberate processes than industrial
design, often they are completely unplanned-for,but they seem to
produce astonishing meta-morphoses of existing designs while retaining the original organization of parts, or classification of
subject-matter. The underlying concept accurately reflects the
context in a way that transcends internal conflicts of design.

COST REDUCTION

We used to say that an engineer is one who can make for sixpence
what any fool can make for half-a-crown. The chief instrument
of the astonishing cost-reductions of mass-produced goods, as
compared to hand-made, is, of course, not ingenuity of design
but investment in tooling-up for repetitive operations. I remember being told, at the Olivetti factory in the early fifties,
that a hand-made prototype of a typewriter that would sell for
£80 had cost £15,000 to build. But, within mass-production,
there are still largish differences of cost and plenty of
examples of big savings made by re-designing the product to
reduce its use of materials, labour, or special-purpose tools.
A formal technique for doing this, Value Analysis, was invented
by L D Miles in the fifties and has been used with notable
success not only to reduce cost but also to rationalize, and
to improve, functional performance. The essence of his method,
which is a lot more involved than this little outline description
suggests, is, as in industrial designing, to focus on function:

          Value Analysis: define element
                           define function
                           consider alternatives
                           evaluate alternatives
                           select best

The strength of the method is that, given that the functions
of each part can be predicted, and held stable, everything
extraneous to their achievement, using the absolute minimum of
resources, can be identified and discarded. But there is a
hidden cost, a severe one, which has only recently become evident.
It is that of inflexibility, over-specialization, the realization
that this 'plastic world' of homogenized, cost-reduced products
is increasingly unalterable, un-repairable, and imposes upon
us (from its stabilization at the larger scale of functions) a
life, an obligatory way of using what is made, that is felt as co-
ercive, not satisfying, with decreasing outlets for individuality.
The lesson is obvious, though how to apply it is not: don't
stabilize functions!

The logic of the components is separated from the logic of their
use by shifting the dimensional grid from walls to joint-positions
and by adding three standardised corner pieces. This change (anal-
ogous to the invention of zero or of the decimal point?) greatly
reduces the number of component types needed and yet allows these
to vary greatly in thickness, material, etc without upsetting the
system.

MODULAR SYSTEMS

Increasingly I find this the most fascinating field of design
and the only one, perhaps, for which I see a long-term future.
Designing at the smaller, and less liberating, scale of products,
functions, seems ready for de-professionalizing. As was writing.

> playing cards
> plugs & sockets
> a cassette
> a brick
> numbers
> the alphabet

Under what conditions _is_ it possible to discover such flexible
and ubiquitous units as these, each system opening up endless
possibilities most of which were unforseen? My own experience
of working with an exceptionally talented designer of modules,
Bernard Keay, suggested that there _is_ an underlying principle:

STANDARDIZATION versus FLEXIBILITY in industrialized
building systems

Our method of resolving this conflict is to maximise the
standardization of joints and to minimise the standardization
of components. This is done by applying modular dimensions to
the _positions_ of joints and by leaving space for _variation_
in the sizes of components that fit into the modular zones
between joint positions.

This was Bernard's way of getting round the fact that, if try to
standardise the sizes of wall sections so that they will join at
the corners of rooms, you need many 'specials' to make up for the
wall thicknesses, which themselves become very restriced. In
this solution, which accepts the use of only three standard
types of corner-piece (L,T,&+) walls can be of any material or
thickness and no specials are needed. The principle, in both
this building system, and in the other examples, seems to be to
separate the logic of the modules from the logic of their use.
Easier said than done. But its not impossible, sometimes.

There is a principle,quite different from that of designing
modules, evident in the type of exceptionally adaptable desk
lamp which is mounted on a spring-balanced jointed arm in which
arm-pieces and springs are positioned much as they are in the
human arm, or leg. The point about this lamp (made in Britain
by Anglepoise) is that the effort to adjust it is less,not more,
than the effort of adjusting your own posture,or eyes, to
continue reading with the light in the wrong place. Many
systems of adjustable components, or so-called flexible designs,
fail at this point. The adjustments they offer are seldom used
because the effort-of-adjusting is greater than that of adapting,
personally or socially, to the worse conditions of leaving the
thing unadjusted. Does this happen with software too?

My last example, and perhaps the most relevant to software design,
is the street, and the street-pattern of a city. Its relevant
because, in both cases, street and software, its the actual thing
itself which is re-used, adapted. A beauty so obvious its invisible.

> Now, after the great war, life goes on in our ruined cities,
> but it is a different life, the life of different or differ-
> ently composed groups, guided or thwarted by new surroundings,
> new because so much has been destroyed. The great heaps of
> rubble are piled on the city's invaluable substructure, the
> water and drainage pipes, the gas mains and electricity
> cables. (Bertolt Brecht, writing of his theatre in Berlin)

The services beneath the streets are, of course, only extensions,
invented millenia later, some of them, of the ancient excellence
of the pattern of streets, and of the so basic idea of arranging
for public space to reach, in this so accessible way, to every
house, no matter how many. A similar example, which is quite
obviously present also in the differnt ways in which computer
storage, and access, is provided, is the library, and the book.
Together they provide equal access times to every book, and to
every page, line, word, letter, by the principle of 'pages', of
splitting an enormously long string of symbols into units each
with access both in series and in parallel.

PART TWO   What can be learnt from the study of design methods?

The formal study of design methods, and the conscious invention
of new methods, such as Value Analysis, Morphological Charting,
Man-Machine System Designing, Brainstorming, Pattern Language,
has been evident for the last twenty years or so. During the
same period there have been new methods, and with them a larger
scale of aims and objectives, in many other fields of industrial
life eg market research, operational research, work study, and
new accounting methods. The common feature of all these
endeavours is, I believe, to enable larger groups of people,
specialists and sometimes non-specialists, to work and think
together on the evolution of industrial life, as a whole, or
in larger chunks than is possible with the more solo methods
they replace. In the case of designing, the typical solo methods
are the back-of-the-envelope-sketch (for the chief designer
at the stage when he keeps the whole problem to himself,
before it is farmed out in pieces to the designers of details)
and the scale drawing (for the detail-designer, working with
a smaller perceptual span but with greater accuracy, geometric-
ally at least). The new methods imply a less hierarchical way
of subdividing the work than do these two solo methods, or
tools. Often there is group thinking <u>before</u> the 'concept' appears.

What I am doing here (using the same technique of writing to
prepared pages, each with its title and example pre-typed) is
to think, not about individual methods, but at some of the
recurrent questions of design procedure that seem to be particularly relevant to the business of trying to make software
that is easy to modify, or of modifying software that isnt easy,
perhaps is muddled by the inevitable unpredictabilites of this
new field of design, with its enormous complexities at the
scale of thought (the largest scale there is?).

In reviewing the new thinking about design I am attending not
so much to specific methods as to the mental and organizational
difficulties that arise when designing reaches outside the
range of experience of any one person, and of everyone.

DESIGNING IN A CHANGING CONTEXT

Imagination, I realised after writing that about'designing
outside the range of experience',has no bounds. That is why
the seemingly impossible, eg to try to design software that
is easy to maintain and modify, is a reasonable thing to attempt.
My first move, when faced with designers or students who feel
overwhelmed by 'the problem' is to ask them to release their
imaginations by attempting not one design, but three: 'A', an
immediate improvised answer, doable this week, or month, or

        What IS the context of design? I seem to have two answers:
        it is our minds, our lives, as persons, as beings able
        always to imagine, to perceive, to remember, and to be,
        beyond the range of whatever others (who may try to serve
        our need or to control our behaviour) can foretell;

        it is also 'evolution', the so slow, and seemingly mindless
        evolution of all things, natural and artificial, which so
        often seems to exclude the 'most rational' or 'most intell-
        igent' actions and to encourage what looks like sheer
        stupidity.

(I forgot the example was coming up: but it seems to fit what
I'm thinking) 'B', a design at the normal time scale, and 'C',
a far-out design, for say ten years hence, assuming that people,
as well as technology, are going to change. The essential point,
in this way of releasing one's mind, is that of seeing how
temporary, and subject to the existence of what is already
designed, are 'reqirements', 'functions', and the like. For
instance, in designing a school building,its folly to tailor
the whole thing to present teaching methods and problems when
its obvious that , in say fifty years of the building's life,
education is going to change quite a lot. What kind of school
will make it easier, not harder, for tomorrows teachers, and
pupils (if those categories still exist) to reorganize according
to how it is then? 'It' being their minds.

PARTICIPATION OF CUSTOMERS & USERS IN DESIGNING

One of the main adavantages of the newer design methods is that
they make the process of designing sufficiently visible, and
discussable, for customers and users to contribute to it the
experience and insight which can only be got at the receiving
end, but not in the design office. However, in the case of
software, the designers are not only the makers too: they are
much more able than are designers in other fields to experience
for themselves, at a terminal, the effects of what they are
doing. But the professional designer of software, despite
this immediacy of trying out his work, lacks the experience
of being adapted to the design he is testing and of being able
to perceive it in relation to the life-activity of which its
meant to be a part. This can be an advantage, for it is just
this condition of being over-adapted to what exists that makes
it difficult, sometimes impossible, for users to help designing
very much. They are adapted to accepting, not to imagining.

As soon as John Suter told me his ideas for leaving a lot
of the designing of houses to the builders, and to the people
who will live in them, I felt he'd begun to do what seems to
me to be most needed in architecture now : to get beyond
functionalism.

John Suter is one of the first architects to have the courage
to attack this difficulty head on. I wrote that note after
being inspired by his account of how, after much encouragement
from him, the family and friends of his client had gradually
begun to take real advantage of the freedom he'd given them
to do for themselves the things that everyone believes 'only
a professional can do'. His role, once he'd given up part of
the design function to his clients, became, as he said, that
of professional encourager. You can do it. Just try. But
he was disappointed to find how hard it was to shake them from
the ideas of functionalism, the accepting of the activity-names
given to spaces and rooms at the start as final, for the life
of the building. Its so hard to unlearn, and unlearning is
the essence of designing. To share the design process with
users is not as easy as it sounds. It needs a change of roles,
of self-images, on both sides.

DESIGNING AS PROCESS

The difficulty which we all face, as users of all the things,
products, or whatever,that are provided by professions other
than our own,is that we are tied by our experience as consumers
of products to accept them, and not ourselves, as the starting
points of our thinking when asked to define our needs. And,
as professionals in the provision of software, or of some other
product, we are equally tied to thinking of the product as
central and the users as existing only in relation to what we
provide. 'We are here to help the others : what the others are
for I've no idea'. That is product-thinking, the not always
laughable weakness of industrial life. The alternative view,
to be found in the recent developments in design, as in all the
arts and sciences of this century, is process-thinking. To see
process not as a means but as the end, a purpose in itself. To
take the product alone as the criterion is to deny that we exist.

> at a break in a concert a most un-announcer-like voice,
> presumably a member of the orchestra, sitting some way from
> the mike, says "we will play the finale - opus one, number
> two"

That was the first occasion, in years of listening to the output of
professionally organised radio, when I have felt the existence of
the musicians as persons, as one of them improvised that announcement, presumably in a rare failure of the official announcer to
keep track. That tiny lapse, in the almost totally impervious
homogenaity of a planned professional service, is I believe the
clue for getting out of the trap of means-ends thinking that
makes us blind to our needs outside those of serving the system.
The essential first step is to accept the roughness, the un-prof-
essional character, the reaction 'that's not design, anyone could
do it' of improvised initiatives by users themselves, by us as
we are as persons, unspecialised. Once this big jump is made
then the way is open to becoming able to making this new life
that is so rapidly coming into being as a result of our efforts,
into something worth while in itself. In computing, more than
in other technologies there is the opportunity to drop product
thinking, to let the process come alive to us all.

DESIGNING WITH CHANGING REQUIREMENTS

The instability of requirements is perhaps the biggest difficulty
in trying to design, and re-design, computer software as it
grows in scale and in length of life. How does it arise? Hard
to say, difficult to predict. My strongest impression is that
the direction in which requirements are going to change, both
during initial design and later, is not predictable from what
either the customers or the clients know at the start.

> The sponsor's brief is treated as a starting point for
> investigation and is expected to be revised, or evolved,
> during divergent search....(but not without the sponsor's
> agreement).

That quotation is from the central chapter of my book on design
methods in which I was describing how the new methods differ
from the traditional ones. The main difference is that the
new methods begin with formal ways of researching the problem
more widely than the client's brief suggests so that the interdependancy of problem and solution can be properly explored
and understood. It is far from easy to perceive, in any
instance, why and how the initial requirement-statement can
be so misleading and that the actual requirements, if the
design is to be good, must reflect what is learnt as designing
proceeds. But it easy to see that, in principle, designing is
a highly informative process (essentially one of <u>unlearning</u>
what we thought <u>was</u> the case, but is <u>no longer true</u> when we
have changed the situation by making something new which inter-
acts with what was there before) and that it is wise to act
always on the latest available information. 'If we'd known at
the start what we've learnt while designing it, we'd never
have done it like this'. The practical point, in using the
newer design methods to make possible collaborative divergent
search,before the reqirements are fixed, is to change the
basis of the contract between designers and clients. Both
parties have to give up the use of the requirements as a semi-
legal basis for control and measurement and to agree to work
together in the continuous meta-process of evolving the brief
and sharing in the eventual decision as to how the problem is
to be seen and solved.

CONTROLLING THE GENERALITY OF SPECIFICATIONS

In teaching design, at the wider scale we are discussing here,
I have always been surprised to see how difficult it is to
write specifications in a way that helps the design process
rather than hinders it. It is hard to keep in the background
of one's thoughts some wider stability which might enable you
to find the level of generality that would be useful.

GENERALITY	VERIFICATION
Ontological	By agreement, negotiation, perhaps force.
Logical	By logical consistency or inconsistency of statements.
Scientific	By objective observations ie independent of who makes them.

This little table is one such background-thought. It reminds
us that differnt kinds of statement, and context, require
different kinds of verification and warns of the folly of confusing these categories. Ultimate objectives, eg is it good or
bad?, are always in the first category and we cannot expect any
certainty of proof that they are rightly chosen. Instrumental
objectives, contributing to these, may involve the seeking of
a consistent logic between means and ends. They may also involve
getting out of one's armchair and looking closely at the relevant aspects of the world. It is always tempting to concentrate
on whichever of these categories one is used to working with
and to neglect the others. Often one's job-description does
not permit one to operate freely at all three. I dont believe
that designing, at the wider scale, can be done well until
everyone is free to think and act at all three levels. But,
at a more practical scale of actually finding the words in which
to specify something, there is another background-thought that
may be useful to many. If you want to know if a given statement
is at the level to be useful to the persons for whom its meant,
ask two questions: does it give them enough room for manoevre
to be imaginative? and do they have the means to know if this
requirement, as stated, has been satisfied?

SPLITTABILITY OF DESIGN PROBLEMS

The essential difficulty, and the attraction, of designing, is
that the problem cannot be split,while it is at the formative
stage, because of the underlying interdependancy of problem and
solution. Each way of stating the problem, no matter how abstract-
ly, implies some range of solutions, and each solution creates
a different world,different needs. At this most challenging
level of designing the process requires conceptual integrity,
wide awareness, detailed knowledge. Yet, for such collaborative
and quick-changing activities as software design, this has often
to depend on many minds, not one. My picture of the degree to
which design problems can be split between many people is this:

SPLITTABLE eg chemical plant (one-to-one relation of parts/
functions)

UNREPETITIVE eg cars, buildings (unified)

KNOWN

UNSPLITTABLE

REPETITIVE eg roads, beams (automatable)

NEW eg first aeroplane, xerography, modular system
(need-creating, contextual)

Splittable problems, and those known types of unsplittable
problem for which an algorithm exists, can be solved by what are
sometimes called glass-box methods, wholly rationally, needing
no imagination to discover the right form. Of the other two
types of problem, unrepetitive known problems require some
degree of black-box method, relying on the imagination as well
as on reason, while new problems require not only both of these
faculties of the mind but also a meta-ability, that of being
able to design the design process while also designing the design.
Software designing, I guess, can be of any of these types.
Splittable, in this classification of mine, means shareable
between several people who are working largely out of communication with each other. Unsplittable means they are acting with
one mind.

It is our tradition, in modern life, to believe that creative
work cannot come of several minds, only of one, and only then
if the person is specially gifted, a genius as we say.

> Men and months are interchangeable commodities only when
> a task can be partitioned among many workers with no
> communication between them. (Frederick P Brooks, Jr.)

Our other common assumption, as Frederick Brooks implies here,
is that the rest of us, not being geniuses, are fit only to
work on farmed-out sub-problems and that, when we do so, the
problems of keeping in step are either non-existent or can
be dealt with by informal communication which need not enter
seriously into our planning and logistics. If we are to solve
the large and increasingly interactive problems of today, both
of these assumptions, patently wrong as they are once you
think about it, will have to go. One has only to look back
to the remarkably coherent results of the highly collaborative,
and unmanaged, process of craft evolution to see that, when
opportunity for communication is ample, and when the effects
of each action can be made evident to all concerned, then it
is possible for creative work to come from a group. There are
plenty of examples in modern life, too, both in computing and
outside it, of amazing achievements which owe more to collaboration
than to genius. The secret is to organise the process so that
each person is acting as much as possible adaptively, creatively,
and that we minimise the need to work to rule, shutting the mind
to the evident effects of what one is doing. Where a top-down
concept has, at some stage, to be accepted, it should, together
with its reasons, be debateable at length by all who will have
to act on it. Frederick Brooks gives a vivid account, in his
book, of how such 'debating the bible' can be organised when
designing an operating system. But I feel myself that, sensible
as his account sounds, there is probably a better way to be
found, one that owes something to the accepting of the incredible
results of unplanned local adaptiveness that is evident in
both natural evolution and in such human processes as craftwork
and the finding of new ways to use modular parts, words, etc.

ERRORS AND TESTS

Perhaps the most important ability to develop in designing is
that of being exceptionally sceptical of one's own ideas,
especially those which occur at the start, while not losing
the capacity to proceed with the problem despite the initial
absense of an organising idea of what the solution is likely
to be. This is where the new methods are particularly helpful,
in that they provide many different ways in which one can
find enough confidence, in what lies outside the problem-as-set,
to be able to proceed in a state of creative doubt. The purpose
of the initial stage of divergent designing, common to many of
the new methods, is of enabling many to collaborate in this
process of discovering what is open to change as the work
proceeds, and what is not. Thus it becomes easier to find ways
of adapting to, instead of obstructing, the aspects of the
problem which must be left undecided for as long as possible
if disastrous errors and back-tracks are not to be forced upon
everyone at a later stage.

> When all is said and done, however, I still advocate
> building a pilot system whose discarding is planned.
> (Frederick P Brooks, Jr.)

That our experience of what existed before the new design was
made, and our capacity to imagine in detail how its going to
operate, are never equal to the complexity and unexpectedness
of what evolves from our designing, need not stop us if we
hold both to a right scepticism of our initial ideas and to
these wise words of Frederick Brooks in which he recognises
the need to formally acknowledge our awareness of the incomplete nature of the thinking that precedes the making of
a new design. Our rationality is always bounded by what
we have already known, needs always to be doubted, put to
test, when we are attempting to create the new. Allowing time
for this, and money, is a start. Enabling all who are concerned
in the process, and its effects, to themselves learn to use
this caution, this imaginative conservatism, is more difficult.
It is something we have yet to do.

PART THREE   How does this apply to the designing of software?

My first thoughts of how this little journey through some of
the possible precedents may help the process of designing,
and re-designing, software, are these:

Contexts
Context (a name I prefer to environment, because it sounds less
like a separate thing from ourselves) is the hardest thing to
perceive, because it includes us, our ways of thinking. The
fish cant see the water. 'It' is the source of change, of
unexpectedness, the real generator of newness, design, of
evolution. Aims, purposes, requirements, functions: these
are words for how we see what's needed. But when we name
them we tend to exclude the main part, the least predictable:
ourselves, our minds, and how they change, once we experience
something. Its ourselves, not our words, that are the real
purpose of designing. The biggest mistake is to take the
product alone as the aim. Its always secondary. Always a
means, to process, to what we're doing now or will be doing
later. Dont compromise the process : get it right.
The best kinds of evolution we know, natural, linguistic, hand-
crafted, are planless but highly responsive to change of
context. With astonishingly coherent results.
The first step to attempting something similar in design, in
continuous designing, is, I think now, to acknowledge publicly
from the start that when we design our knowldge is of necessity
incomplete. And to design the design process to reflect that
modesty, that expectation of learning what the problem is as
we try to solve it, discarding first thoughts. To make the meta-
process sensitive to what is learnt in the highly informative
process of designing.

Functions and parts, ends and means
Functions, statements of requirements, are essential but temporary.
Without them we cannot begin, but unless we can change them we
cannot finish, cannot discover. The essence of natural and
linguistic evolution is to adapt parts, existing parts, to new
functions, disregarding the old ones. This almost miraculous

process is possible only when the context is mobile, is sensitive
to the new functions of existing parts and is not tied to the
old functions. This, the largest scale of change there is,
supposes fluidity, not fixity, at its most abstract level, at
the scale of aims, ends.

So, for continuous designing, dont stabilise functions. To fix
the functions inhibits the human adaptiveness, present in
everyone, but inhibitable, upon which longlife designing depends.
Hard words. Its difficult to see how, in software designing
it can be done. In the short term its expensive because function-
fixing is the basis of cost reduction. But in the long term
mobile functions should be the real economy, the way to enlist
the efforts of everyone to smoothing the way.

How to fix the concept, how to get clarity, conceptual integrity
as its sometimes called? Imposed top-down is useless, unless
one can design a break between the concept and the parts. The
right concept has to embody a true perception of what is
mobile and what is relatively stable in the context, and it has
to embody this insight in a way that is independant of internal
design conflicts. Thats the challenge to ingenuity.

How, in practice, to cope with changes in requirements and
specifications? First, recognise that the 'right' requirements
are in principle unknowable by users, customers, or designers
at the start. Devise the design process, and the formal agreements between designers and customers and users, to be sensitive
to what is learnt by any of these parties as the design evolves.
Organise collaboration so that each person concerned has (a) the
liberty to experiment and improvise and (b) the means to test
his or her improvisations to the operation of the whole. The
extent of (a) and (b) may vary much from person to person but
must always be such as to prevent destructive change, or the
making of blocks to other changes.

Built-in adaptiveness, is it possible? Yes. But its the most
difficult kind of designing there is. Designing modules is a
process very hard to describe and theorise about : its mind
operating close to limits. There seem to be a few guidelines.
Separate the logic of module-combination from the logic of
use (which may require the invention of extra parts eg the
decimal point). Let the sub-parts be capable of independant

adaptation to context changes. Ensure that the energy needed
to adjust the design is less than the energy needed to adapt
oneself to a worsening situation of using it unadjusted.
Make access routes equal regardless of size or number of things
to be accessed.

Collaboration and communication

Creative collaboration is perhaps the main challenge of our time.
Before computing it was not possible, in principle, at the scale
at which we now operate and organise. The scale of billions and
at the scale of everyone's minds. Its bound to be difficult
but it is, I believe, the hidden question behind the quest for
longlife designing. The attempt to act together as if all the
things we make comprise one thing, a unity. As we do ourselves.
But a unity that leaves us incredibly free, to make or mar.
What are the blocks to collaborative design? What stops us
acting together as a context for our works, adapting freely to
what we discover in doing what we do? The blocks are product-
thinking, function-fixing, role-fixing, cost-reducing, and our
identification of ourselves with these things instead of with
our thoughts, feelings, minds, common-sense awareness of what
is needed but what we're not paid to do. All this leaves us
over-adapted to the status quo (which we identify with self,
with security, when in fact its what destroys the self, the
being, the joy of living). Thats why, I believe, we seem to
lose the adaptiveness, the biological adaptivness, with which
we are born. The first practical step to unblocking, to being
free to be inventive, and collaborative, is to widen, and to
overlap, our job specifications, our roles. Once that happens
the whole context begins to become mobile.
As larger groups begin to work together in design we need not
only looser roles but more public ways of thinking aloud. More
visible design processes so that everyone can see what is being
decided, and why, before, not after, the main decisions are
made. Collaboration before concept-fixing is perhaps the main
strength of the new design methods. The other strength is
to provide means of unlearning, publicly, with changing, not
fixed, self-images.
Attentiveness to context, not to self-expression, is the

skill we have to foster, to encourage, to share. In natural
evolution inattentiveness is death. So is inability to adapt
to what we see happening. The context, not the boss, has to
become the manager of what is done, and how. The bosses role
becomes that of designing the meta-process, designing the
situation so that designing collaboratively is possible, so
that it flows.'It' being the interaction of what everyone is
noticing with what everyone is doing. To find out how to re-
structure the design situation so that the blocks are removed,
so that initiatives are both encouraged and enabled to be self-
correcting, given attentiveness, and the right tools, etc.
A first step is to change the contractual basis of collaboration
between designers, customers, users, all concerned: make it
independant of functions, requirements. Find some better
level for agreements.
How, in principle, is the context, the design situation, to be
organised if all this is to be possible? The general aim is
to enable all concerned to take initiatives in the light of
accurate knowledge of the effects of what they are doing. In
practice this sounds very difficult. To make a start I'd
suggest beginning by loosening specifications so as to allow
'unprofessional' degrees of roughness to be acceptable in
improvisations from any quarter and to consciously drop professional standards wherever they seem to have local, not
universal importance. Secondly I'd try progressively to do
away with the need for 'forced communication', via manuals,
meetings, memos, etc, and try more and more for the kinds of
collaboration-without-communication that is possible in the
evolution of language, in the use of modular systems, etc.

Now that I've finished these first thoughts about what are
the main lessons to be learnt from other fields of design
and evolution, and from design methods, I can see that they
are a very tall order, a counsel of great perfection. And not
at all easy to take in, expressed, as they are, in very
abstract words and phrases. I hope that, in the course of
the conference, after some other minds have had a go, that
this line of thinking will become clearer, more concrete.

216
REFERENCES

J Z Young, <u>An Introductionto the Study of Man</u>, Oxford University
Press, London, Oxford, New York, 1971.

Owen Barfield, <u>Poetic Diction, a Study in Meaning</u>, Faber and
Faber, London, 1928. (still in print)

George Sturt, <u>The Wheelwright's Shop</u>, Cambridge University Press,
Cambridge, London, New York, Melbourne, 1923. (still in print)

L D Miles, <u>Techniques of Value Analysis and Engineering</u>, Mc Graw-
Hill, New York, 1961.

Bertolt Brecht, <u>Collected Plays, Vol 5</u>, editied by Ralph Manheim
and John Willet, Vintage Books, Random House, New York, 1972.

Frederick P Brooks, Jr., <u>The Mythical Man-Month, Essays on</u>
<u>Software Engineering</u>, Addison-Wesley Publishing Company, Reading
Mass., Menlo Park, Cal, London, AMsterdam, Don Mills, Ontario,
Sydney, 1975.

J Christopher Jones, <u>Design Methods</u>, John Wiley & Sons, London,
New York, Sydney, Toronto, 1970.

The quotations not cited as coming from the above publications
are from my recent writings some of which are published by
Princelet Editions, 25 Princlet Street, Spitalfields, London,
E1 6QH, and Postfach 780, CH 8025, Zurich.

The tabulation of splittable and unsplittable problems is a
version of what is written as prose in Design Methods. The
diagram of it was worked out by Juan Bonta and appears,
slightly differently,in his article in a spanish language
publication: El Simposio de Portsmouth, Editorial Universitaria
de Buenos Aires, 1969.

Vte. MARTINEZ DAMIA
PUZOL (Valencia-España)
R. E. n.º 12.157 **CAT. II**

5

de 60 a 75 m/m

Cebollas LIRIAS

Linda

things

This was written in response to a letter from Th. Laffineur, editor of Neuf, a journal of architecture, urbanism, design and construction which is published in Belgium. Later I discovered that two of the co-editors, Monique Bucquoye and Georges Patfoort, whom I had met while teaching at the school of industrial design at Antwerpen, had suggested that I write it. It was published in Neuf, volume 4, number 87, in the summer of 1980, with an introduction in Flemish and French written by Monique. It is reproduced here by permission of Socorema S C R L, Rue de Merlo 28, O 1180 Bruxelles, Belgium.

dear editors of Neuf,

You asked me to write a text
for the special issue of Neuf
on the theme 'artefactica'.
I've not seen this word before
and note that you have chosen it
because
of the recent misuses of the word 'design'
and
'its close connection with the consumer society'.
(Is it bad to consume? Is it bad to eat?
Perhaps you mean that it is bad to be forced to consume
to satisfy the desires of others
to produce,
and to profit from producing,
from working,
from designing too?......)

I also have had objections to the word
design
feeling that it has become more a matter of control
than of trying to improve the world.
(Is it possible to improve the world?......
I'm reminded of what was written on this question
by John Cage,
from whom I've learnt so much in recent years.
He wrote:
'Our intention is to affirm this life, not to bring order out
of a chaos or to suggest improvements in creation, but simply
to wake up to the very life we're living, which is so excellent once one gets one's mind and one's desires out of its way
and lets it act of its own accord.')

So,
with these various objections
to the word design,

and with your new word artefactica in mind,
I am writing about 'things',
the things themselves,
rather than the intentions of their designers.
And I will try to complete this text
without using the word design
any more.
That will be a new experience for me
and I hope interesting to your readers.

You asked too for illustrations.
I have chosen eight 'things'
to be illustrated:
a room, a chair, a tv, a car, a book, a city, a phone, a brick.
I will now go and buy a film
and photograph examples of such things
the ones I find around me
here in London this July.
Then I will send you the photos
to be inserted into the text,
which will consist
of my thoughts
on being confronted
by these artefacts
these 'things'
that have somehow found themselves appearing
in this article.
Elements of this place,
of my life here,
little pieces of the world,
as we make it.

To take this photo of the room where I am writing this text
(you can see it on the typewriter)
I had to stand on the landing outside:
the room is so small.
Its small because I get cold when I write
and this is the cheapest room to heat in the daytime
when everyone else is out
and the central heating's off.
I suppose its the oil producers,
the OPEC countries,
who have forced me into this
the littlest room
in a big house.
My big working room is now unused
except for storing books and papers and things.
We call it 'the messy room'.
It is.

As I looked into the room
to take the photograph
I realised that
while writing at the window
I am almost unconscious of the room, as such.
What I'm aware of
is the view, the street, the house across the road,
the people passing by,
the trees, the clouds, the light......
and the items close to me:
the keyboard, the text I'm typing,
and what I'm thinking of.
And I'm conscious of the chair, the things I reach for,
pens, papers, books, etc.

I become aware of the room behind me
only if someone comes in.......

And when I adjust the heating, ventilation, light, or curtains,
to suit the continual slight balance-and imbalance
of my body temperature, and eyes, and posture,
and the changing weather and sunlight or cloud or rain or dark,
outside,
I become momentarily aware of this thing, this 'room'.
I like it very much,
this little writing-place,
this frontier,
between
the in-and-out,
the thoughts, the words, the pressing-of-the-keys,
as life goes by.

It was built as a dressing-room,
in 1900,
there are doors, unused, on each side of me as I write,
to the bedrooms on either side,
one of which is now a bed-sitting room, a studio, for Joanna,
a type of room they may not have known
when the house was built?

The bentwood chair.
Some kind of classic, rethought, brought up-to-date,
and trendy now,
obligatory almost,
for those of us who live
what we take to be the modern life?

Why the cushions?
I chose the chair because the profile felt right
in itself
without such extras
(having spent many years researching the comfort of seats
and being able, I thought,
to pick a chair that would be comfortable
in many hours of sitting).
But I was wrong.
This chair too is inadequate for that,
perhaps because,
in typing,
one is leaning forward such a lot?

(I notice, in writing this, that this having-to-comment
on my chair
is pulling me
out of the unconscious don't-bother-me-with-such-thoughts
attitude
of the active 'user'
into the aware-and-interested attitude
of ther ergonomist, the thinker, the 'observer'.
Its showing once again
how true it is
that
once you are involved in something
you lose sight of what it is.
'If I knew what I was doing
I wouldn't be here.')

The armrests,
I notice now,
are worn, bear the marks of use.
Yes. That's right. I use them a lot.
Not only to rest my arms but enable my arms to hold up my head,
not having a strong table-top to lean my elbows on.
(I prefer to put my papers on an inclining, adjustable, table
of the kind used in hospitals
for reading in bed.)
Its not good, I fancy, to be holding-up-your-head
all day long.
The neck should do that,
along with all the other things it does.

*

TY FILM 5063

→7   →7A

To take this one I sat in the best chair for viewing tv
in the room downstairs
a chair that's exactly the right distance
(the distance at which
each side of the screen
lines up with one's first and fourth knuckles
when one's arm is outstretched;
that's a figure I took from tv viewing research
done by the Ford Foundation
twenty years ago
but still true, I guess,
the eye and hand being 'things' that do not change).

But what am I saying?
The eye is NOT a 'thing', an entity,
and neither is the 'hand'.
Cut them off from the body
and they cease to work, to operate,
they die.
This whole idea of 'thing'
of artefact,
is wrong,
as is any 'naming', any treating of parts of the world

as seperable entities.
The whole purpose
of the new thinking of recent decades,
thinking about 'systems', 'environments', and 'integration',
was to recognise that:
the interconnectiveness of life,
that which is alive, not dead.

We've begun to forget
that great advance
of the fifties and the sixties.

On the screen as I watched: horse riding competitions.
Something I hate in actual life
but
when on tv
I watch it, often.
Why IS that?
Some strange compulsion of the screen,
a major element of modern life,
twenty hours a week for many,
equal to the hours spent in class
by a every schoolchild.
Do we know what we're doing?
If we did
would we be here?

The VW Beetle.
The German 'people's car', of 1933 or so,
still going very strong
a real classic,
advanced thinking when it was conceived,
and now loved for itself,
as 'a thing'
as something worthy in itself?

This one is my daughter Sarah's car,
parked outside the house,
her first,
she has a degree in philosophy
and is unemployed
finding it hard to get a job.
Nobody wants a thinker,
so it seems.
Why is that?
A philosophic question?

What is a car, what IS a car?
Do we know what it is?
I'd say it is MOBILITY,
the freedom to move,
at will,
without planning,
over a wide area,
the area of 'the city', 'the country', 'the continent',
no longer tied to walking-distance,
to village, farm, or tribe.
The freedom to exist,
as an influence, a person in touch,
over half the world.
A real magic carpet.   One wish, and you're on your way!

John Cage's life
described in a book
by Richard Kostelanetz
(published by Allen Lane, London, 1970).

The book from which I copied the quotation at the start,
photographed here, just as I'd put it down,
on my tilting table-top.

What an influence, this book, all John Cage's books,
as far as I'm concerned.
The books which have REALLY influenced me, or so I think.
(For the last ten years I've been working quite largely
along lines learnt from John Cage,
with his idea of composing as being 'not control'
but 'letting things happen',
and I've also been following the example of his friend, and mine,
Edwin Schlossberg, from whom I've learnt much else,
too much to mention here,
of what he calls 'as is',
and living in the present,
or trying to......)
THE BOOK,
sometimes, I think,
the prime technology,
the most dangerous of all,
the medium through which we channel all our public thoughts
before they are allowed
to be realised in other forms,
as for instance objects, broadcasts, systems, or whatever.
Time we forgot the book a bit, I'm sure,
and trusted once again to word-of-mouth,
and the look in the eye,
and stopped requiring signatures, certificates, credentials,
and all this 'education',
meaning years-and-years,
of reading-and-writing what our elders thought and did.
What's so good about that?

How to photograph THE CITY?
Looking round the room, and into the street,
and thinking 'do I have an air photograph of London?
no I don't,
and besides
the air-view is not the city as we experience it,'
I realised that there is no place,
no single place,
no THING,
you can truly call the city.
The city is what's happening,
simultaneously,
in so tight-packed an area,
involving so many people,
all operating as one thing,
one inter-connectivity.
Its the connectiveness that is the value of the thing,
that's the reason for the high rents for city space,
and why,

if you want to live cheaply,
'for a song' as we say, so beautifully,
you'd better find a cottage in the wilds
far from any road, or water-main, or drain,
and far from any neighbour,
let alone the city lights......

Once I got downstairs I saw the answer:
photograph the Evening Standard, the London daily!
Which I did,
noticing the headlines:
£10-pound-a-night lure for tourists,
LONDON BARGAIN HOTEL DEAL
(which refers to a new scheme for airlines to help standby pass-
    engers
to book cheap beds
in London hotels
provided they are willing
to leave their holiday plans
to the very last moment).

I like that:
'the last moment'.
Isn't it just what we need, now?
To drop all this planning for a bit more action
and excitement?
(What an incredible hotel,
its not what I'd have chosen,
but who knows?)

SAVE OUR CITY
says the slogan also visible.

This moment,
as I write,
four men are moving a piano
out of the house across the road
and into a van
which is called Tiger Trucks.

The lady I've seen living there for years,
but whose name I do not know,
seems to be moving out.
Where is she going? I expect I'll never know.
City life.

*

The telephone. My favourite technology,
the only big communications-medium that is decentralised,
in which the messages,
unlike those in newspapers, or in broadcasts,
or in most of the big systems of which modern life consists,
are not planned from a central office.
(Mail is of course decentralised too,
but I'm thinking chiefly of electrical systems.)
And what messages! So trivial, so important,
who can say which,
and so personal, so improvised, so close to life-as-lived,
as-loved,
and so far from regimented, planned, dragooned,
unconsidered-in-advance.

Twenty years ago,
in my articles on Automation and Design

(I've had to break that promise not to use the word)
which appeared in the magazine Design
(there it goes again)
I was amazed, and very glad,
to find,
in the elements of the telephone-system,
a prototype
of the elements of automation
(invisible central mechanisms, not controlling the functions,
and operating automatically,
visited only by craftsmen, when things go wrong,
and widely distributed in-out devices,
the telephones as we see and touch and listen to them,
each adapted well to human body and action
and
despite operating via a mechanical flow of impulses
imposing no mechanical constraints upon the things you say
and listen to....).
Writing those articles taught me a lot
taught me to reverse my opinions of the new technology
the technology of complexity
and to see that it is no longer inhuman
in any inherent way.
Only the old technology of simplicity-and-power,
the coal-and-iron machines, and factories, and such,
are things to fear.
In the new machines and systems
the fear,
if it remains,
comes not from the machinery
but from ourselves. Our distrustful uses of things.

I notice also in the photograph
that I felt impelled
to include what stood beside the phone:
my index cards of phone numbers and addresses.
These remind me that perhaps the most novel element
of 'the telephone'
are the numbers which we get,

and take as almost-names,
in order to be able to communicate.
And I'm reminded that
in the more rigidly ruled countries
its said they do not issue directories to everyone,
the majority of numbers being unlisted, secret,
ex-directory as we say.
I'm also reminded that John Cage,
though beset,
like many celebrities,
with midnight calls from freaks who only want to hear his voice,
insists on keeping his number in the public book.
'The book'. That's the way to use it, openly,
and why, no doubt, its feared:
the power of the book,
the accessible word,
made semi-permanent.

*

My last 'thing', the brick,
or rather several bricks comprising now a piece of wall,
by the kitchen door.
I'm hoping that the photo will show the irregularities

of the bricklaying
which reveal how
in this craft
unorganised by any mechanical control-system
there is a subtle process
or errors-compensating-for-errors
as each brick is laid
'deliberately wrong'
in its position and direction
so that the resulting wall
(not itself so much a 'thing' as an ideal concept of flatness)
is accurate, within narrow limits,
while the bricks themselves
are none of them in their 'true places'.
This is only one small example
of the subtlety
the essence of life-human, life organic,
which in our earlier industrializations
is lost.
But resurrectable,
if we look for it,
and rethink our later, more flexible technologies,
on the same lines.

The brick by itself is,
I believe,
the most easily conceived example
of a type of product, artefact,
which,
unlike so much of what we make,
opens up possibilities
instead of closing them off.
Think of all the buildings
and uses of bricks
there have been in the world so far.
And think of all the other uses of this unit, this 'module',
which are yet to come.
We cannot.
The variety is too great for any single mind, or life.

238

And so it is with the other 'modules' that we use each day:
the words, the letters, the numbers, the plugs-and-sockets,
the nuts-and-bolts, the microchips, the lightbulbs, the
canisters, the tyres, the envelopes,......
These,
I believe,
are the models
for how,
in our present doubts about design,
to re-invent 'the thing', the artefact, the world.

* a slice of these photos was removed to fit page-format of Neuf.

never say oh dear said Mrs. Reynolds because there is no use in
saying oh dear and said Mrs. Reynolds if there were any use in
saying oh dear, oh dear said Mrs. Reynolds and she said how do
you do and good-bye to Andrew Ell, and she knew she said she knew
and she did know just what it would do. Every month makes it
just that much earlier that is makes the night come just that
much sooner. Mrs. Reynolds could always believe everything there
was to believe.
  Mrs. Reynolds went away and then she went home.

Gertrude Stein
Mrs. Reynolds

4

THINGS OF AUGUST

is designing a response to
the whole of life?

Wolfgang Preiser wrote to me in 1973 asking if I would present
a paper at the conference of EDRA (the Environmental Design
Research Association) at Blacksburg, Virginia. The story of
how I reacted against the abstract language of such conferences
by writing a conversation of different voices appears in two
earlier essays (How My Thoughts About Design Methods Have
Changed During The Years and "......in the dimension of Time.")
The chance process by which it was automatically composed consisted of taking a random number to find which of the five
voices would speak next and then typing the next sentence from
a text written by that voice (for the texts by Stevens and
Jung, which were being copied out consecutively) or else by
taking another random number to find the page and an imperfect-
ion on that page to find a spot on it (for the texts by EDRA,
Kant and Whitman, which were being copied out in random sequence).
Nothing was left to the decision of the writer once the choice
of the voices and texts had been made. The role of writer, or
composer, becomes, as John Cage says, that of "a listener" no
different from that of anyone else. Christopher Crickmay has
provided an account of his listening, or interpreting, which
includes several points which I would never have thought of,
as might the interpretation of anyone else. I like very much
this removal of the originator, or professional, as a screen
between the composition and those may attend to it or "decide
what it means", to them.

Graham Stevens, whose account of inventing 'inflatables' appears
in the play, came with me to the conference and brought it to a
standstill with his demonstration of 'walking on water' (inside
a large plastic balloon on a nearby lake). Graham's inflatables,
more so than those of others, are the closest to being works of
pure art. Some of them, the most beautiful and fleeting, last
only for hours or minutes as vast enclosures and surfaces of
transparent film float on water or in the atmosphere, making
visible the winds, the currents, the pressures and continuities
of the medium in which we breathe and move. I asked him to
re-enact his story of how his inflatables came into existence as
his straighforward account seemed the best thing I could find
to contrast with the abstract behaviouristic theories of design

against which I was reacting at the time. At the performance
of the play I invited various people (who seemed to me to in
some way resemble the writers of the texts) to read the voices.
Graham read his own, Tom Regan read for Walt Whitman, Ada Esser
read for Kant, Wolf Hilbertz read for Jung, and I read for EDRA.
Each of us stood at different points in the audience as pictures
of the writers and of Graham's inflatables appeared on the screen.

I am grateful for the permission of Graham Stevens to reproduce
his account, which appeared first in Art and Artists of May 1972,
and for permission to reproduce the photomontage, to Christopher
Crickmay for permission to reproduce the text Dreams and Reason,
and to Messrs Dowden Hutchinson & Ross Inc for permission to
reproduce the essay which first appeared as "Is Designing a
Response to Life as a Whole?" in ENVIRONMENTAL DESIGN RESEARCH,
Volume 2, edited by W. F. E. Preiser, Copyright © 1974 by Dowden,
Hutchinson & Ross, Inc., Stroudsburg, Pa. Reprinted by permission
of the publisher.

The phrase 'reason can dream what dreams cannot reason' which
Chris Crickmay quotes comes from the poem 'I have all the time
in the world, my world' by Nicholas Snowden Willey in his book
The Green Tunnel, published by Signals, London, 1965.

The essay was published in Spanner 17, Aloes Books, London, 1979.

IS DESIGNING A RESPONSE TO THE WHOLE OF LIFE?

An imaginary conversation between EDRA, Graham Stevens, Immanuel
Kant, Carl Jung and Walt Whitman.

Composed automatically by a chance process at the request of

J Christopher Jones
The Open University
Bletchley, Bucks, England.

Abstract

When EDRA told me that I was to speak on "Design Languages and
Methods" I remembered having once written that

> "methodology should not be a fixed track to a fixed destin-
> ation but a conversation about everything that could be
> made to happen. The language of this conversation must
> bridge the logical gap between past and future but in
> doing so it should not limit the variety of possible futures
> that are discussed nor should it force the choice of a
> future that is unfree."

This conversation is hardly possible while the language of
design theory remains so narrow and machine-like so I have employed a chance process to compose a wider but imaginary conversation between five voices: EDRA, an artist-designer, a psych-
ologist, a philosopher and a poet.

Introduction

The voices in the conversation are as follows:

> EDRA speaks some randomly chosen titles from the Conference
> program,
>
> Graham Stevens tells, in his own design language, how the

idea of making inflatable environments came to him in a flash,

Carl Jung[2] speaks a paragraph he once wrote about method,

Immanuel Kant[3] speaks sentences randomly chosen from his "Critique of Pure Reason",

Walt Whitman[4] speaks randomly chosen lines from "Song of Myself".

I chose Kant because there is such a similarity between the language of design theorists and that of his philosophy. (Someone once said Kant's writing is illuminating but difficult: it should be read first for the fourth time.) I chose Whitman because I love his exuberant American vision and because it contains so much of what is missing from our own writings.

The chance process, which decided who should speak next, and which chose statements at random from the texts, is adapted from the way John Cage[5] composes his lectures.

EDRA   Implementation of strategies leading to environmental change.

STEVENS   During 1964-65, I spent a year with other students organising a movement to change our educational system, culminating in the Stockholm Students' Symposium passing a resolution that students should have full participation in all aspects of their education: selection, assessment, course content, lectures, etc; it also passed a resolution that exams should be abolished.

EDRA   Gaming and simulation

STEVENS   With all these negative aspects it seemed necessary to start from the beginning - from nature, the body, and people's behaviour; investigations into what was needed and how it could be done.

JUNG: An ancient adept has said: 'If the wrong man uses the
           right means, the right means work the wrong way'.

STEVENS: The relevant aspects of the course being studied were
           given by Professor Page on environmental physics, which
           also included the physics of the body; G. Broadbent on
           the theory of design, including the creative process
           and kinetic art.

EDRA: Design languages and methods

KANT: I shall, therefore, restrict myself to the simple and
           equitable demand that such reasoners will demonstrate,
           from the nature of the human mind as well as from that
           of the other sources of knowledge, how we are to proceed
           to extend our cognition completely a priori, and to
           carry it to that point where experience abandons us,
           and no means exist of guaranteeing the objective reality
           of our conceptions.

WHITMAN: I have instant conductors all over me whether I pass or
           stop,

WHITMAN: At the cider-mill tasting the sweets of the brown mash,
           sucking up the juice through a straw,

WHITMAN: And peruse manifold objects, no two alike and everyone
           good.

KANT: Now, as every principle which imposes upon the exercise
           of the understanding a priori compliance with the rule
           of systematic unity, also relates, although in an in-
           direct manner, to an object of experience, the principles
           of pure reason will also posess objective reality and
           validity in relation to experience.

WHITMAN: Divine am I inside and out, and I make holy whatever I
           touch or am touch'd from,

WHITMAN: Approaching Manhattan up by the long-stretching island,

WHITMAN: There is no stoppage and never can be stoppage,

KANT: It is evident from the remarks that have been made in
         the preceding sections, that an answer to this question
         will be far from being difficult or unconvincing.

JUNG: This Chinese saying, unfortunately all too true, stands
         in sharp contrast to our belief in the 'right' method
         irrespective of the man who applies it.

STEVENS: These studies, coupled with experience in painting,
         meditation, rock music, slum housing (I was deeply
         dissatisfied with the current architecture, its limited
         concern with small sections of the environment, its
         rigid unresponsive, immovable demand that people might
         adapt to their environment instead of having it adapt
         to them) led to the Spacefield project.

KANT: But this representation, I think, is an act of spontaneity;
         that is to say, it cannot be regarded as belonging to mere
         sensibility.

JUNG: In reality, in such matters everything depends on the
         man and little or nothing on the method.

EDRA: Implementation of strategies leading to environmental
         change

WHITMAN: The connnoisseur peers along the exhibition-gallery with
         half-shut eyes bent sideways,

KANT: We cannot even cogitate time, unless, in drawing a
         straight line (which is to serve as an external figur-
         ative representation of time), we fix our attention on
         the act of the synthesis of the manifold, whereby we
         determine successively the internal sense, and thus
         attend also to the succession of this determination.

WHITMAN: This the touch of my lips to yours, this the manner of
yearning,

STEVENS: Spacefield assumed immediate importance in the way in
which it brought together and unified all the other
isolated experiments and interests, at the same time
answering the dissatisfaction with architecture.

JUNG: For the method is merely the path, the direction taken
by a man.

WHITMAN: Adorning myself to bestow myself on the first that will
take me,

EDRA: Decision making tools

WHITMAN: I will go to the bank by the wood and become undisguised
and naked,

KANT: For, granting that certain responsibilities lie upon
us, which, as based on the ideas of reason, deserve to be
respected and submitted to, although they are incapable
of a real or practical application to our nature, or, in
other words, would be responsibilities without motives,
except under the supposition of a Supreme Being to give
effect and influence to the practical laws: in such a
case we should be bound to obey our conceptions, which,
although objectively insufficient, do, according to the
standard of reason, preponderate over and are superior
to any claims that may be advanced from any other quarter.

KANT: Transcendental freedom is therefore opposed to the
natural law of cause and effect, and such a conjunction
of successive states in effective causes is destructive
of the possibility of unity in experience, and for that
reason not to be found in experience - is consequently
a mere fiction of thought.

JUNG: The way he act is the true expression of his nature.

KANT: For if they are to have something more than a mere logical
        significance, and to be something more than a mere anal-
        ytical expression of the form of <u>thought</u>, and to have a
        relation to <u>things</u> and their possibility, reality, or
        necessity, they must concern possible experience and its
        synthetical unity, in which alone objects of cognition
        can be given.

JUNG: If it ceases to be this, then the method is nothing more
        than an affectation, something artificially added, root-
        less and sapless, serving only the illegitimate goal of
        self-deception.

WHITMAN: Give me a little time beyond my cuff'd head, slumbers,
        dreams, gaping.

JUNG: It becomes a means of fooling oneself and of evading
        what may perhaps be the implacable law of one's being.

STEVENS: Its particular form was mainly derived from a piece of
        tactile sculpture made in 1965, designed to express the
        idea of containment - fullness, emptiness, filling and
        emptying, texture, weight, volume of content, etc.

KANT: For, as in the former case the cognition (conclusio)
        is given only as conditioned, reason can attain to this
        cognition only under the presuppositions that all the
        members of the series on the side of the conditions
        are given (totality in the series of premisses),
        because only under this supposition is the judgement
        we may be considering possible <u>a priori</u>; while on the
        side of the conditioned or the inferences, only an in-
        complete and <u>becoming</u>, and not a presupposed or given
        series, consequently only a potential progression, is
        cogitated.

EDRA: Quatitative techniques in environmental analysis

JUNG: This is far removed from the earth-born quality and

sincerity of Chinese thought.

STEVENS: While considering these properties, the nature of toy
balloons assumed greater importance.

(EDRA'S instructions were to complete the paper in 5 pages or
less,* so I decide here to silence the other voices so that Graham
Stevens has space for his story. JCJ)

STEVENS: The idea of the balloon as a flexible, tactile skin,
completely expressive of containment, simply came in
a flash while I was walking down a street.

Balloons were filled with water, soap solution, salt,
beads, etc., and when air was used, one became much more
aware of air as a material, with its own kinetic properties.

The whole exercise was immediately popular with the
people around, with its range of sexual and humourous
connotations - people squeezed, stretched, rubbed, poured,
and ejected water and soap solution, swung, dangled,
threw, made noises, sucked and passed around the balloons
from one to another.

Knowing very little about the technical aspects of air
structures and having seen photographs of warehouse-type
structures, the Space Field project had to be worked out
using models, discussions, contacting high-frequency
welding equipment manufacturers and making up the
structure in borrowed factory space over a weekend.

This was done by a process of trial and error for
determining fan size, material thickness, amount of
wind-loading, on-site repairs, anchorage, creep; until
finally a week later, failure then success showed what
kept the structure up or down, and anchored to the
ground. Through this experience, the nature and

*This re-typing of the text, being more widely spaced, occupies
more than 5 pages.

potential of the air structure, beyond that of storage
function, became apparent.

References

1. Stevens, Graham, Blow-up, ART AND ARTISTS, May 1972.

2. Jung, Carl Gustav, THE SECRET OF THE GOLDEN FLOWER, (Translated by Wilhelm, Richard), Routledge & Kegan Paul, London,
   1962, p. 83.

3. Kant, Immanuel, CRITIQUE OF PURE REASON, (translated by J.
   M.D. Meiklejohn) Dent: London, Dutton: New York, 1934.

4. Whitamn, Walt, LEAVES OF GRASS. New American Library of
   World Literature (Signet Classic), New York, 1954.

5. Cage, John, SILENCE, M.I.T. Press, 1966.

WALKING ON WATER

WATERBED 1966   TRANSMOBILE (Pat.'67)   WALKING ON SEA WAVES   PONTUBE (Pat.'67) with
WATERBOOTS 1969   HOVER PALLET IN HOVER TUBE (Pat.'70)   low and medium pressure.

(photos: forrest, kilburn, ogden, stevens, tweedie)

DREAMS AND REASON: an interpretation of the imaginary
conversation between EDRA, Stevens, Jung, Whitman and Kant.

C.L.Crickmay   30.3.73.

(In this note a writer attempts to find meanings new to him in
the spaces between the contrasting voices of a conversation
composed by chance. This interpretation is not meant to be
believed by others except as a record of what the writer (C.L.C.)
thought while reading the paper. The chance text is intended to
be open to different interpretation by each individual reader or
member of the audience.)

A first look at the text reveals how consistent are the statements of Jung and Whitman with the account of Graham Stevens.
Together they appear to invalidate the voice of EDRA altogether,
and reveal Kant as sterile. Stevens' story fits exactly Jung's
description of a method as "merely the path, the direction taken
by a man". His account of sources "painting, meditation, rock
music, slum housing", his integration of all these and other
experiences by starting with balloons, and his interest in the
experience for its own sake; "people squeezed, stretched, rubbed,
poured and ejected water and soap solution" fit exactly Whitman's
joyful assertion of total sensory awareness, "I have instant
conductors all over me whether I pass or stop", renders impotent
Kant's typically Western struggle to grasp totality via the
intellect.

A second look reveals a dilemma which I interpret from Kant's
statement "For, granting that certain responsibilities lie upon
us, which, as based on the ideas of reason, deserve to be respected and submitted to, although they are incapable of a real
and practical application to our nature, or, in other words,
would be responsibilities without motives, except upon the supposition of a Supreme Being to give effect and influence to the
practical laws: in such a case we should be bound to obey our
conceptions, which, although objectively insufficient, do,
according to the standards of reason, preponderate over and are

superior to any claims that may be advanced from any other quarter".

Our reason tells us, says Kant, that we have responsibilities which lie outside our personal motivation. Perhaps it is not practical to live permanently in a Stevens-Whitman-Jung-like world. The practical world is sustained by rational processes of which EDRA speaks. However, and here is the crux of it, we are not bound to reject the practical world as mere necessity, if we suppose that it contributes to a wider purpose than that of which we are conscious. I am reminded of one theme of Mailer's "Fire on the Moon" in which he speculates that the landing of men on the moon, a triumph of EDRA-like rational strategies, may still be a part of a total flow of things of which we are unaware.

Perhaps this is the meaning of Nicholas Snowdon Willey's paradoxical phrase 'Reason can dream what dreams cannot reason'.

I have one doubt about this second interpretation and that is to do with machines. There is a strong possibility that the practical life, of which Kant speaks, could one day become exclusively the realm of automatic machines. If this is the case, then the actions of Stevens and the words of Whitman and Jung refer to our future and EDRA refers to the future of machines.

35 wishes

By 1976 writing conference plays had become a habit. This one
was composed by improvisation rather than by systematic chance
process, out of events, readings, phrases spoken by others or
heard on the radio while I was typing. I believe that the
experience of accepting words given by a chance process had
taught me to be much more accepting of words from any source,
including those from my own thoughts which formerly I'd have
rejected as unsuitable in some way. Below standard. Much of
the process of composing and performing this play is evident
in it. The whole thing is performed: title pages, instructions,
the initial abstract, everything.

About six months before the conference I was asked by Frank
Height and Christopher Cornford to send the abstract (the page
beginning 10.10 am Wednesday 14 April). A day or two before
the conference I visited the exhibition which was being got
ready for it and copied down 35 phrases from the captions to
photographs and other exhibits of 'designs for need'. Slightly
edited these became the recipie for Utopia with which the play
begins. The page beginning DESIGN FOR NEED ! was composed out
of words from the conference programme. The play itself,
starting at the page titled 'after 35 wishes THE SCHOOL OF NEEDS',
was composed by imagining what a typical day, or night, might
be like if all the promises implicit in the exhibition had
been kept and the world was freed of problems, as seen by designers. To write it I merely kept including in the text events
happening around me while referring to the theme of the conference and to lines from texts that were to hand. I imagined that,
in any Utopia, one would be completely unconscious of the problems
which had been solved by its designers and would be struck by the
similarities to ordinary life under any conditions, utopian or
not. One would still be preoccupied with such questions as when
to go to bed, what to read, where to go, what to eat, what to
say to someone, and probably unaware that the air was clean, the
housing shortage was solved, and poverty eliminated, etc.

The play was performed, or rather read, by Shiu Kay Kan and
Michael Poteliakoff (who were exhibiting 'the tin can house') and
by Vicky Cowell (the press officer and an amateur actor) and
myself. With music and props. And pauses. At chance intervals.

35 wishes

a performance
composed for the design for need conference
at the royal college of art, london, april, 1976

composed with the help of:

        chance processes
        the imaginary rock foundation
        the conference exhibition
        frank height and christopher cornford (persuaders)
        edward blishen's book,"the school that i'd like"
        muriel spark's book "the mandelbaum gate"
        kenneth koch's book "wishes,lies and dreams"

        and and many others particularly my family and and

DESIGN   FOR   NEED !
NEED !

a major international symposium
with supporting exhibition

to examine the present and the future
contribution of design
to
the satisfaction
of social needs

book now to be sure of a place

the numbers are strictly limited

10.10 am Wednesday 14 April   John Christopher Jones

35 wishes

As I write this note I am composing this paper (its not likely
to be a lecture) and so far know only the title.
When Frank Height asked me to speak I replied with a letter
saying that I'd much prefer to attend a conference at which
designers did not display what they had done, or proposed, for
those in need, but instead assisted users to say in public what
their needs are. And perhaps helped them to design their own
solutions. Christopher Cornford asked me to be more constructive
than that, and to speak for 35 minutes. I was reminded of the
book"The School That I'd Like"by Edward Blishen (Penguin, 1969)
in which schoolchildren answer this question. Gillian,15,begins
the book: "The school I would like would be perfect,glorious in
every way...." and it ends with Nigel,14: ".....Let us rebel,us
the opposed,and cast out those wage pulling civil critizers and
form our own schools. The which teach us the beauty of all rough
and tidy. Please excuse the spelling,no one will educate me."
Hence the title.   35 minutes to say what we want.

What wishes are implicit in the conference programme?
          THE EARTH: I wish I had a friend
          SEWAGE: I want to be food again
          THE HOUSE: I want to be autonomous
          INDIA: I wish I had no problems
What's missing? These don't seem to be the right wishes. What
would life FEEL like if all these wishes came true? That's my
question. 35 minutes: to see and hear what our utopia would be,
a composition of our dreams.

UTOPIA

when somebody is hurt an ambulace comes
our fundamental needs (flirting,feeding the hens, cutting the
corn) have been satisfied (what do we do now?)
the population explosion is over
we no longer depend on ever more sophisticated techhnology
we have stopped exhausting our planet's resources (whose?)
design problems have ceased to be complicated
we are not noisy now
the anti noise campaign has succeeded
the old kent road flyover is used for roller skating on sundays
we have alternative transport systems
all planners use the symbol language
i live in an eco house
we have a bicycle made for two with better social disposition
(side by side)
bad management has been cured (by MORE management)
the oil boom is over
our community is fully developed
we have been rehabilitated
we have decimal housing (DECIMAL housing?)
we live in a tin can house
we have low energy houses
all domestic waste is saved
housing is available for everyone
alison has a wheelchair
i can hear the talking newspaper
we no longer need to search all bags and parcels
we are not committing future generations to problems we can't handle
we're not in this for the money, we're in it for life
neccessity is no longer the mother of invention
we have stopped using machine language (have we?)
there is no more pollution (none)
handicaps are no longer handicaps
we have agreed the future
everyone is taught design
people count
there are no more poor countries
there are no more rich countries either

after 35 wishes

THE SCHOOL OF NEEDS

sir !
this is a design
you mean the words
no   the time   35 minutes   that's how long it takes

ok   we'll do it

it hasn't started yet

THE SCHOOL OF NEEDS

would you like a cup of tea
mmmm
what's the matter have you got a headache
no my neck is stiff
i can't stand this
one moment you're prostrate and the next you're tapping away
i was waiting for an idea
a cup of tea
if i'd have known that i'd have brought you one
i didn't know i wanted it
I was waiting for something to happen
lights a cig
no need to say your wishes
reach for them
the audience waits
corrects typing errors
reach for them
22 spaces
you gave me one
he goes to get it
empties it
woman
eleven o'clock   the church clock strikes
i can hardly hear
he was in bed   now he's typin
spark   muriel   what's she got to say
on a pilgrimage to the holy places
she clears her throat
of jordan, barbara vaughan, half jewish
it's up to the performers to decide which are the words
and which the stage directions
while performing
so it's different every time
barbara embarks on a pilgrimage
that becomes a rout
a desperate adventure of abduction and espionage

do you mind this tapping
no
a switchback of tragedy and farce
a love story, sacred and profane
cover photograph by van pariser
a woman with dark hair
the bes piece of furniture in the room was the camp-bed
and barbara lay upon it
cough
awake
gazing straight through the small window
and who DESIGNED IT
at the night sky
THE SKY
which
by contact with her emotional eyesight
was elated
with stares and lyrical energy   energy
that's what we're short of
who
that's an insult to the sun
S U N
that would put an end to the gossip
pulling it to pieces
life
what was the point
what was the point
the point
oint
t there's a t missing   the best piece
he rubs his chin again, nobody knows why
we know what our needs are
don't we
don't we
this is the school
the ideal
the ideal school
the ideal home   that's not a home   it's an exhibition
he stands up to look for something

the book
two minutes a pge   a page
that's a typing error
how much is error and how much is life
now you're being philosophic
why not   why NOT
it was underneath the other book
the unreal one
no, not unreal, it was a book too
but the wishes were unreal
wishes lies and dreams
in all the millions of words that are written annually
about education
one viewpoint is invariably absent
how does she know
that of the child
the client
its not at all difficult
to think of another sphere of social activity
a SPHERE
the earth
?
?
in which the opinions of the customer are so persos tently over-
                                                           looked
sis
who MAKES the errors
the unseen intelligence?
in a light airy room
i find chris, the lecturer, already seated
the stage directions
chris tells of research into the life of king george III
throwing light
catch
not to make fun   what we say is us
on the latter's fits of insanity
what a bore school is nowadays
no need to act it
i don't like it when the first few minutes tell you

what all the rest is going to be like
no tea left
she's sleeping
repeat page one[+]
and again[+]
no more[+]
what was the idea of this play   if it is a play
just to provide some composed experience
any
the words don't matter
but they're selected carefully
what about the wishes
thirty five
many thanks
for your 35 wishes
i want to be autonomous
not THAT   what is it anyway
this is a design   the play is a design
no
its the thoughts of those who watch it that's the design
and they are indeterminate
and much more extensive than what i'm writing here
here is not here
on the page
where is here
there
what ARE your needs then   what are they
your needs
all you can do in that building is what the designers expected
in the old one you can do many things
its time we danced
i have some terrible wishes
o that's not terrible   it's nice   don't we all
o
he wanted everyone to enjoy his wallpaper
as he enjoyed cycling in the country and looking at the leaves
utopia?
here's another cup of tea
do you want some toast

[+]the page beginning 'would you like a cup of tea'

```
no     do you want some
no     i won't bother
did you need to buy that car
i don't want to talk about that
I'M GOING BACK TO BED NOW
are you coming
mmmmmmm
you need me
this could go on for ever
is this utopia
this
this
this is a committee meeting
what's on the agenda
for the future
the future can be perfect     perfect
come off it kid
we're living in the future     how's it feel
the royal college of the future
the conference
art'n'design
A'N'D
i need bringing up to date, i've had this hairstyle for tears
that's not a need
no
no
mmmmmmmmmmm     mmm
she works as a secretary AND looks after her husband and junior
junior
yes, junior
you know
i know nothing
nothing
yes     i mean no
where's barbara gone
she went out
is that a need
all kids are equal
nobody is average thuogh     though
```

how do you pronounce that
there are moments when i wonder why i'm sitting here
but this is the conference of your dreams
our dreams
dreams, like wishes, are a frequent source of poetic inspiration
has the post come
there weren't any
none
but it's her birthday
he goes to look again
dreams, like wishes, are a frequent source of poetic inspiration
even the scary parts
ooooooooo
the planning of extraterrestial communities
the same problem
for instance
the navajo universe consists of mutual relations
between several types of beings
humans animals supernaturals ghosts and natural forces
ooooo
yes   that's a nice word
i'm thinking of using it
using it
yes
mmmm
yes
what for
o   i don't know
i like it
yes
in the US house most of the space is taken up by furniture
or by space
not much be people
the night chant dance of the navajo
takes nine days to perform
the step used throughout
used
yes used
is a type of trotting step, performed thusly

thusly
yes   it's a nice word
i hate it
hate, that's not a subject for us to discuss here
a thing of beauty is a joy for ever
why were you tapping in the night
typing
i was writing a play
you gave me the idea

pause*

that was a red pause

black pause

nobody nobody
has decided
what you are thinking what ARE you thinking
no need to apologise
for utopia
for you

NO MORE PROBLEMS:

ebeneezer (a shorthand writer): it is deeply to be deplored
        that people should continue to stream
        into the cities

        he invented the garden city

        how to combine the fundamental vividness
        the fundamental vividness
        of rustic life

* red ribbon

        with urban culture
        that is the main problem

        of the EVOLUTIONIST
        him
this is utopia
not a committee meeting
or a discussion
it's a slice of life
fiction
perhaps you came for something
yes
icame i came
thinking of your daughter
i cannot speak for her, let her say
this is the custom
if she is willing , there are no further formalities
in Zuni
it is never thought to be difficult
men are perenially willing
to aquire a new husband
she gathers his possesions   and places them on the doorstep
his skirt, his shoes, his precious feathers, his paint-pots

pause

music

he comes home
it is evening
he picks up the bundle   and returns to his mother's house
it is the subject of only fleeting gossip

bickering is not liked and most marriages are peaceful

the client speaks
the neglected client   the user
is ther a user
there

here
we are here to solve problems
we are here to help the others
what the others are for i've no idea
this IS th school of needs
the school
where we learn
social needs
not otherwise being fulfilled
this seems good   good

pause

these pauses can be inserted anywhere in the play

all the actions are very slow

this pause is timed
to make the play exactly 35 minutes long

the play continues
he looks at his fingers
she continues
distributing the wealth   that's ok

no more dissatisfied clients

have you any serious wishes
those are the context
35 of these are to made public during the performance
the wishes of the audience
noted beforehand

and presented   as faits accompli   as if they've happened

now i'm going
to look for her: if she sleeps   that's good   good
chopin piano music throughout   and liszt
off and on

the scene is composed to
the scene is composed
to be seen
with wishes incorporated
                          and perhaps the night chant
                          dance music (track 1 folkways
                          album fd 6510)
performers:
each marks his or her words in one colour in the text
some to be spoken some to be acted some both

wishes:
could be prerecorded on the tape with the music
could be indicated by slides notices or scenery or extras
 public needs, one's own needs, deep, superficial, constructive,
 destructive, any

what are extras
anything that is added
that's progress
progress is no longer a question of destroying the present
to make room for the new
its just adding to what is here
extras

in the spirit of

the present
this is a present

 it hasn't started yet   (end)

. . . .

Words, phrases, and occasionally lines from the following
sources are embedded in the play, here and there:

Edward Blishen's book The School That I'd Like, published by
Penguin Books, Harmondsworth, 1969.
Muriel Spark's book The Mandelbaum Gate, published by Macmillan,
London, 1965 and Penguin Books, Harmondworth, 1967.
Kenneth Koch's book Wishes Lies and Dreams, Teaching Children
to Write Poetry, published by Vintage Books, Random House Inc,
New York, 1970, originally published by Chelsea House Publishers,
1970.
Ruth Benedict's book Patterns of Culture published by Routledge
and Kegan Paul, London, 1935, and much reprinted.
Magoroh Maruayama's article Design Principles for Extra-Terrestial
Communities, in Futures, volume 8 number 2, April 1976.
The record sleeve of the American Indian music, Folkways Album
fd 6510.
A text by Ebeneezer Howard.
A play by Tedeuz Kantor.

voices at the
conference conference

Most of what I might say about this essay is included in it.
Of those written through a chance process this is perhaps the
only one in which I regretted or doubted some of the statements
appearing and edited them somewhat or expressed my thoughts about
them. I would like to thank Anthony Judge for inducing me to
make notes for a paper about conference design and to Barrie
Evans for persuading me to write the essay, long after the
conference at which I spoke had finished. Its first publication
was in the conference proceedings: Changing Design, edited by
Barrie Evans, James Powell, Reg Talbot, published by John Wiley
& Sons Ltd, Chichester & New York, 1982, pages 347-367.
The following note, written a year or so before the essay, was
prefaced to it.

. . . .

28 March 1977
Suddenly, after days, years, of worried seeking, planning,
and not finding: release.
I realised that, of the things done before, the ones that were
done with ease, lucidity, were not the ones that tried to achieve
anything, or to change the world, or to improve my lot, or anything like that. They were things like just writing out thoughts,
out of curiosity, to see how they'd go, and things like sculp-
ting, and attending to the thoughts and sensations, existentia,
while inspired or otherwise enthralled, by some artwork or
composition, some theory, or such.
They were not things like plans, ideas for how the world of men
could be improved, not even the lighthearted plays and stunts
made in protest. Neither were they any acts of protest or
rebellion or deliberate change of circumstance. Not factional
at all.
So?
A signal at last to just stop trying, to realise there is
nothing to be got or gained, only something to be free of:
anxiety and an obligation to do what "should" be done. If there
IS any necessity, of acting for others, eg to earn, it should
also be, if at all possible, a way to enjoy doing that, or doing
whatever is not chosen but brought by circumstance.
The middle-life change at last: the learning to accept, and to
be free in accepting. What is.
How fortunate if this indeed is happening.

NO SHOULD
ONLY IS

That poem, sent me by Edwin Schlossberg, he thought I needed it,
to whom my thanks, again, a gain.

VOICES AT THE CONFERENCE CONFERENCE

Earlier this year I was invited to speak at a conference about
conferences but it never took place. Now I have been asked to
write a paper about "context designing", a concept which I
mentioned at the Portsmouth Conference but did not explain.
Instead I gave an example of it by reading John Cage's Lecture
on Nothing, a composed talk that is meant, like a piece of music,
to be performed to a tempo and thus to be not so much a message,
meant to control our future thoughts and acts, but an experience
of the moment in which we are freed from the anxieties and
purposes that often close the mind to all but self interest.
A context in which our thoughts may be unexpected not only to
the lecturer but to ourselves, the audience.

Today I do not want to repeat, in writing, that lecture which
is better heard than read (and which is available in John Cage's
book Silence) so I am trying to compose something in the same
spirit to exemplify context designing and perhaps to explain the
idea too, if that is possible. It seems to me that I can do this
by bringing together some thoughts on the designing of conferences, thoughts of others as well as myself, as all such
"softwares" as conferences, courses, computer systems, legal
systems, political systems, public services, societies, groups,
communications and the like are more contexts than products and
all suffer the marks of neglect, total neglect, by the imagination, the artistic mind, the impulse to make life beautiful.
These fine things, what are proudly called creative processes,
seem so far not to have been applied to the shaping of industrial
life itself but only to the shaping of the hardware and the art-
works, the products not the processes. Is it possible to design,
to make pleasant, beautiful, not only the results of industrial
and human processes but the conditions in which these processes
occur? To get rid of alienating ways of acting and communicating
and rule-making and planning and instead to make new forms of
industrial life in which the millions, and billions, of us who
now exist can feel everywhere at home? That is the serious
question before this play.

Who is to speak (at this conference-on-the-page, this account
of a discussion that never took place, this play in my mind,
and yours, as we read between the lines of what is said)?
The first to arrive is Shih Nai-An, Mr SHIH, a Chinese gentleman
from the thirteenth century, perhaps. He is not able to listen
to what the others are saying so long after he has left this life
so he will be speaking the words he wrote in introduction to
Water Margin, the book of stories that he wrote to entertain
himself and others in the absence of his friends. He came to
my mind because his description of friendly conversation seems
to me the best I've read, amusing and beautiful, even though
today he would be called an enemy of the people. This paper is,
I suppose, about the possibility that our enemy, as people, is
ourselves, as non-people, as ciphers, roles, as specialists
deaf to thoughts and feelings. Able to see that the system's
wrong but not free to put it right. We only work here. He
begins to speak by himself before the others come. He speaks
his mind. For anyone to read. He has the time, long past, to
think about the future.

MR SHIH:
A man should not marry after thirty years of age; should not
enter government service after the age of forty; should not have
any more children after the age of fifty; and should not travel
after the age of sixty. This because the proper time for those
things has passed.......

He is interrupted by the arrival of INTERNATIONAL MAN, a busy
fellow, expert at attending conferences, that is his life. He
is not happy to hear that the proceedings have begun without
mention of the agenda, the official programme of topics to be
discussed at this conference about conferences. He begins to
read from his list of 82 ideas for those unfamiliar with
international conferences so that they may become efficient and
satisfied participants.

INTERNATIONAL MAN:
Discretion is all very well, but timidity is useless and annoying. Remember that others are in the same position as you,

and may be even more isolated. Introduce yourself to other people and make as many introductions as possible between other participants.

MR SHIH does not hear this interruption and continues speaking. We do not hear what he is saying as INTERNATIONAL MAN speaks in a loud voice. Those who want to know what they missed can read in J H Jackson's translation of Water Margin (The Commercial Press Ltd, Hong Kong, 1963) the words we did not hear.

MR SHIH:
..........Why talk about insects when the whole world is before you? How can you count time by years? All that is clear is that time passes, and all the time there is continual change going on. Some change has taken place even since I began to write this. This continual change and decay fills me with sadness.

He falls silent. It is the end of a paragraph. I wonder about this old-fashioned dislike of change and for a moment hear the ghost of Edmund Spenser flit by offering to speak his cantos on change, Mutability as he called it, or was it her?, trying to prove all things are subject to decay. But Mutability was defeated, in Spenser's mind, by Mother Nature who, at the point of defeat, argues that change is not decay but growth in which each thing works its own perfection, approaches its true state of being. At which she, Nature, vanishes and Mutability is seen to be subject to perfection. The doctrine of progress, now so discredited with us, how far is that a fallen version of that hope of man, of Edmund Spenser, and of what was once the modern spirit? But, sympathising a little with the desire to get on with things, and to leave philosophy aside, I leave Spenser to return to his time. For the present.

Others arrive, all ready to begin speaking, so I decide its time for some order if everyone is to get a hearing. Order? Isn't that, our idea of order, what's wrong, what's so ugly, what's making progress (the life industrial) so unpleasant, unjust, alienating? I feel that there is no official view of order that

282

permits anything but distrust to organise the lives of everyone
alive, now that we are so numerous. So, without asking if he
approves, I adopt a form of order preached and practiced by John
Cage, the order of chance, an attempt to get as near as can be
got to unintentional designing, not presupposing an aim except
that of "imitating nature in her manner of operation" while
trying to set aside self-interest. Is that possible? I don't
know but it seems adequate to me: to let a chance process
(letting a random number table decide who speaks and what they
say) be the organising principle. And thus to exhibit some
trust in what is outside one's conscious purposes. Numbers 1 & 2
will be the signal for MR SHIH to speak another sentence from
his book; 3 & 4 for INTERNATIONAL MAN to speak whatever of his
82 ideas is chosen next by random process; 5 & 6 will permit
THE WRITER (me) to speak, initially from a short piece I wrote
in 1973 about designing a conference and, if that source runs
out, to improvise some responses to what the others say; 7 & 8
will enable us to eavesdrop on JOHN CAGE reciting sentences
chosen randomly from his Lecture on Nothing; 9 & 0 will bring
quotations from what THE DESIGNERS (Nigel Cross, Robin Roy,
Reg Talbot and myself) wrote about in our report about the
future of confernces in 1969. MR SHIH, being the oldest speaker,
will have the last word. The play will continue until he has
reached the end of his piece. By which time I hope that whatever
can be learnt, by myself and other readers, about context
designing or about whatever else is said, will be evident.
(An impious hope, not in the spirit of the design, the play,
the unintentional process?) Who is going to open the proceedings, now that everyone is present?

JOHN CAGE:
Originally we were nowhere; and now, again, we are having the
pleasure of being slowly nowhere.
(He speaks slowly, with long pauses, to a tempo of his own.
The chance process favours him with a request to speak again.)

JOHN CAGE:
There seemed to me to be no truth, no good, in anything big in
society.

THE WRITER:
Henry Sanoff said something that begins to answer this question.
(The question was: what is a second generation design method?
That was the question in 1973.)

THE DESIGNERS:
How much money are people prepared to pay for better facilities?

INTERNATIONAL MAN:
Listen carefully, bearing in mind the aims of the congress, the
views of the speaker, and your own; make notes while listening.

THE WRITER:
He pointed out that the organisers of the EDRA Conferences have
each year tried to make it different from conventional conferences, less ponderous, more human, etc.

MR SHIH:
What excites pleasure in me is the meeting and conversing with
old friends.

INTERNATIONAL MAN:
Don't overstep your alloted time. This may annoy the chairman
and the other participants.

THE WRITER:
But each year it turns out just like every other conference.

THE DESIGNERS:
Delegates may not ask questions because (a) they are timid (b)
they don't know if the question would reveal their ignorance
(c) they don't want to make the author appear foolish in public
(d) they have no questions.

JOHN CAGE:
I myself have called it form. It is the continuity of a piece of
music. Continuity today, when it is necessary, is a demonstration of disinterestedness.

284

THE DESIGNERS:
We hope that better use can be made of the unique opportunity
afforded delegates to technical conferences, the opportunity
to interact with a large sample of co-workers gathered together
in the same place at the same time.

THE WRITER:
"Why, he asked, can't designers design a conference?"

MR SHIH:
But is is very galling when my friends do not visit me because
there is a biting wind, or the roads are muddy through the rain,
or perhaps because they are sick.

THE DESIGNERS:
The main causes of the problem appeared to be as follows:
1 Inadequate information about delegates, papers, etc
2 Over-restriction of the conference schedule
3 Poor quality papers
4 Difficulty of recapitulating on the contents of technical
   sessions.

THE WRITER:
A good question.

JOHN CAGE:
(He rises to speak, remains standing for a few moments, and sits
down.)

MR SHIH:
Then I feel isolated.

JOHN CAGE:
All I know about method is that when I am not working I sometimes
think I know something, but when I am working, it is quite clear
that I know nothing.

THE WRITER:
Since our conversation I keep remembering his words and at last

I have what feels like an answer: "Because they are IN IT"

THE WRITER:
Is it that design skills and methods as we know them are suited only to the designing of objects outside of ourselves and that a new kind of method is needed if the level of designing is raised from that of objects to activities?

JOHN CAGE:
I must say I still feel this way, but something else is happening : I begin to hear the old sounds - the ones I had thought worn out, worn out by intellectualization - I begin to hear the old sounds as if they are not worn out.

THE WRITER:
To design an event of which one is a part, an activity one is going to live oneself, sounds exactly like deciding what to do in life anyway.

MR SHIH:
Although I myself do not drink, yet I provide spirits for my friends, as my family has a few fields in which we grow millett.

MR SHIH:
In front of my house runs a great river, and there I can sit with my friends in the shadow of the lovely trees.

THE WRITER:
So designing becomes a way of ordering life, or re-making a culture while living it.

THE WRITER:
That's as much as I want to quote from what I wrote in 1973. Its time to renew my vehicle licence. How I hate having to search for all those certificates of insurance, log books, etc.

THE WRITER:
In an earlier version of this paper, now discarded, I realised that words and numbers are good examples, perhaps the best that

can be found, of what I mean by context design. Though having a
purpose they are used in ways that are not predictable in advance.
It is as if there is no separation of designing from using: just
a process, or tradition, in which, each time a word, a letter,
or a number is used, the user is free to reinvent its purpose,
to a great or less extent, and also to reinvent its sound or
shape, so long as it is decipherable.

THE WRITER:
New methods cannot force us to do good, nothing can, but they
can change the context of designing. There is a morality in
widening the scope of life; what was inevitable or impossible
before becomes now a conscious choice.

JOHN CAGE:
It is and it isn't.

MR SHIH:
I have four old women to do the cooking and household affairs,
and also ten small boys who act as messengers.

THE WRITER:
All those messengers? Is that your equivalent of having a postal
service and being able to use the telephone?

INTERNATIONAL MAN:
Arrive punctually at meetings.

THE WRITER:
Its time I thought about what has been said. At a conference
that would be difficult but here I have a printout of the proceedings as they happen and can halt them at any moment to review
my thoughts and theirs......I read through from the beginning,
much enjoying the diversity of views, but unable to digest it
all just yet. I like the idea that one reading does not exhaust
this text: that different meanings may emerge at different times,
depending on the reader's state of mind, and how long he is
prepared to ponder what is said. Just now I'm curious to go on
and see what comes next.

MR SHIH:
If all my friends came there would be sixteen, but because of
the weather there are seldom more than six or seven here.

THE WRITER:
I pause to do the last thing needed for the renewal of the vehicle licence: as the registration document was stolen I have to
copy out the chassis number from the vehicle onto the form applying for a new one. I notice that, since vehicle registration
has been computerised, the people seem much more helpful when
you phone the office about any difficulties like this. That's
just what, in the fifties, I predicted would happen as computers
began to take the drudgery out of life. But many people seem
to find that computer systems are making life more difficult.
Why is this?

THE DESIGNERS:
b) profit to venue organizers

A	B	C
=	(+)	(+)

(This is a line from a table showing how three proposed new
kinds of conferences, A B C, affect the interests of the parties
concerned. In this case Type A has no effect and Types B & C
have possible positive effects.)

INTERNATIONAL MAN:
Take advantage of meals, receptions and excursions; change to
another group instead of staying with your compatriots, or at
the same table, or in the same coach.

JOHN CAGE:

JOHN CAGE:
However modern music still fascinated me

with all its modern intervals. But in order to have them
the mind had fixed it so that one had to avoid having pro-

gressions that would make one think of sounds that were not
actually present to the ear. Avoiding did not appeal to me.

THE WRITER:
I dont know what to say.

MR SHIH:
When they come they drink and chat, just as they please, but
our pleasure is in the conversation and not in the liquor.

THE WRITER:
I still dont.

JOHN CAGE:
If anybody is sleepy, let him go to sleep.

JOHN CAGE:
A lady from Texas said: I live in Texas. We have no music in
Texas. The reason they've no music in Texas is because they
have recordings in Texas. Remove the records from Texas and
somebody will learn to sing.

MR SHIH:
We do not discuss politics because we are so isolated here that
our news is simply composed of rumours, and it would only be a
waste of time to talk with untrustworthy information.

THE DESIGNERS:
Seating for only $\frac{2}{3}$ of delegates
(Item from a list of hundreds of difficulties reported by
people attending conferences)

INTERNATIONAL MAN:
If you do have to read a text prepared in advance, because this
is more concentrated in substance than an improvisation try to
avoid the temptation of reading it too quickly. You run the risk
of not being understood by your colleagues or by the interpreters. In any case, you should always let the interpreters see
the text beforehand.

MR SHIH:
We also never talk about other people's faults, because in this
world nobody is wrong, and we should beware of backbiting.

THE DESIGNERS:
Effects of conference evolution on conference goals.

THE DESIGNERS:
Conference Type B is likely to have the benefit (to sponsors
and employers of delegates) of increasing the speed of technology transfer and the penalty of higher cost.

THE DESIGNERS:
In formulating solutions, we have fitted the new types of
conference into an "evolutionary pathway" along which conferences
may develop from their present form to something like that which
we envisage in perhaps ten to fifteen years time.

THE DESIGNERS:
One feature of Type B Conference is a transcript office which
relays a continuous print-out alongside the TV of the proceedings, and from which transcripts may be obtained.

MR SHIH:
We do not wish to injure anyone, and therefore our conversation
is of no consequence to anyone.

MR SHIH:
We discuss human nature about which people know so little because
they are too busy to study it.

THE WRITER:
I'm having to edit the statements of the designers as the chance
process keeps picking out inexplicable statements from long lists
and tables of which the report is mainly composed. Writing in
lists: what does that suggest?

THE DESIGNERS:
Disadvantages of large international conferences:

1) Standard format with little time for discussion, still less for exchange of ideas, comments and criticisms.
(10 items listed)

THE WRITER:
To abandon function, purpose. That could be the releasive step we've yet to make.

INTERNATIONAL MAN:
Remember that quite a few of those listening to you without listening to the interpretation are hearing a foreign language and that many dont know it very well. If you wish to be understood speak slowly and clearly, pausing before and after difficult words. Dont use uncommon terms and avoid quotations and colloquial expressions.

INTERNATIONAL MAN:
If you have any questions, address them to the appropriate authorities; if you do not know who the appropriate authority is, ask at the information desk.

INTERNATIONAL MAN:
If possible, prepare a condensed version of your speech in a few concise paragraphs. The person writing the account of the proceedings will be grateful to you and you will be surer of being reported accurately.

INTERNATIONAL MAN:
Mark on your list of participants the names of those whom you want to meet.

MR SHIH:
My friends are all broad-minded and well educated but we do not keep a record of our conversations.

MR SHIH:
The reason for this is (1) we are too lazy, and do not aspire to fame; (2) to talk gives us pleasure, but to write would give trouble; (3) none of us would be able to read it again after

our deaths, so why worry; (4) if we wrote something this year
we should probably find it all wrong the next year.

INTERNATIONAL MAN:
If the preparatory work of the congress is carried out by meetings of national committees or working groups, take part if you
are invited to do so; get to know their conclusions and recomm-
endations.

JOHN CAGE:
If one is making something which is to be nothing, the one making
must love and be patient with the material he chooses. Otherwise
he calls attention to the material, which is precisely something,
whereas it was nothing that was being made; or he calls attention
to himself, whereas nothing is anonymous.

THE WRITER:
Dear John, I expect you've noticed that International Man is
intent on making a lecture on nothing even though I'm omitting
most of yours?

INTERNATIONAL MAN:
Speak straight into the microphone without turning your head
and keep the volume of your voice as even as possible.

THE DESIGNERS:
Delegates cannot store ideas about papers and listen to the
paper at the same time.

INTERNATIONAL MAN:
Before leaving for the congress check to see whether any working
papers are missing, in which case make a list and ask the congress secretariat for them immediately on arrival when completing the final registration formalities.

INTERNATIONAL MAN:
Keep an eye on your listeners and if you get the impression
they havent understood you, repeat what you have said, if
possible more clearly.

KEEP AN EYE ON YOUR LISTENERS AND IF YOU GET THE IMPRESSION
THEY HAVENT UNDERSTOOD YOU, REPEAT WHAT YOU HAVE SAID, IF POSS-
IBLE MORE CLEARLY.

INTERNATIONAL MAN:
before starting, state clearly and audibly your name and the
organization you represent or belong to, without using any
abbreviations. It is essential to those taking the minutes or
recordings to be able to identify you and to attribute what
you say to the right person in the report of the proceedings.

THE WRITER:
I can't stand much more of this. Why on earth did I invite him?

THE DESIGNERS:
The chairman may favour his friends (or people whose views,
or calibre, he knows) when selecting people to ask questions
during the discussion.

INTERNATIONAL MAN:
If a wireless installation is being used, obtain your earphones
before entering the hall.

MR SHIH:
I have written these seventy chapters of Shui Hu just for my
own pleasure after my friends had left, or when they had not
turned up owing to the weather.

JOHN CAGE:
Much of the music I love uses the twelve-tone row, but that is
not why I love it. I love it for no reason. I love it for
suddenly I am nowhere. (My own music does that quickly for me.)

MR SHIH:
I have had no preconceived plan, but have jotted these items
down just as they occurred to me, sometimes when sitting outside near the bamboo fence, or at early dawn when lying on my
couch in pensive mood.

THE DESIGNERS:
The principal evolutionary features of our solutions are facilities for: 1) improving and increasing the <u>exchange of information</u>, using the conference as a <u>problem-solving</u> device, individual or small group <u>research and study</u>, being able to <u>re-cap on the proceedings</u>, improving and increasing delegate <u>enjoyment</u>. All of these features incorporate or enhance the concept of multi-level participation.

INTERNATIONAL MAN:
Before leaving, check to see if evening dress is requested for the receptions.

MR SHIH:
But someone may ask, "As you did not write down your friends' conversations why have you written this book?"

THE WRITER:
I'm often advocating creative inaction: less doing and more perceiving. But a lot of this is neither.

JOHN CAGE:
Blackbirds rise from a field making a sound delicious beyond compare. I heard them because I accepted the limitations of an arts conference in a Virginia girls finishing school, which limitations allowed me quite by accident to hear the blackbirds as they flew up and overhead. There was a social calendar and hours for breakfast, but one day I saw a cardinal, and the same day heard a woodpecker.

INTERNATIONAL MAN:
(I've lost the list of 82 ideas.)

JOHN CAGE:
(He stands but does not speak.)

INTERNATIONAL MAN:
(I've searched again, not too thoroughly, but he seems to have dissappeared.)

294

JOHN CAGE:

The other day a pupil said, after trying to compose a melody
using only three tones, "I felt limited." Had she concerned
herself with the three tones - her materials - she would not
have felt limited, and since materials are without feeling, there
would not have been any limitation. It was all in her mind,
whereas it belonged in the materials. It became something
by not being nothing; it would have been nothing by being
something.

INTERNATIONAL MAN:

When not using your earphones turn the control to zero so that
your neighbours will not be disturbed by noises coming from your
appuratus.

MR SHIH:

To which I reply (1) because it is just a hotchpotch, and
cannot make me famous or even discredit me; (2) I have only
done this to fill up my spare time, and give pleasure to
myself; (3) I have written it so that the uneducated can read
it as well as the educated; (4) I have used this style of
composition because it was such a trifle.

MR SHIH:

Alas! Life is so short that I shall not even know what the reader
thinks about it, but still I shall be satisfied if a few of my
friends read it and be interested.

JOHN CAGE:

That forty minutes has been divided into five large parts, and
each unit is divided likewise. Subdivision involving a square
root is the only possible subdivision which permits this micro-
macrocosmic rhythmic structure, which I find so acceptable and
accepting. As you can see, I can say anything. It makes very
little difference what I say or even how I say it.

JOHN CAGE:

Originally we were nowhere; and now, again, we are having the
pleasure of being slowly nowhere. If anybody is sleepy, let

him go to sleep.

THE DESIGNERS:

MR SHIH:
Also I do not know what I may think about it in my future life
after death, because then I may not be able even to read it.

INTERNATIONAL MAN:
Please speak clearly - however quick the reactions of the interpreters may be, it takes several seconds for them to absorb your
idea and to express it correctly in another language.

THE WRITER:
The boy told the teacher what was wrong with his teaching. The
next day he was teaching as the boy had advised.
(The writer pauses to think, conscious that some new principle,
perhaps obvious once seen, named, but hidden as yet, seems to
be sought and needed in this conversation, in the world of
design, in the life we live......our context.)

JOHN CAGE:
I have a story: "There was once a man standing on a high elev-
ation. A company of several men who happened to be walking on
the road noticed from the distance the man standing on the high
place and talked among themselves about this man. One of them
said: He must have lost his favourite animal. Another man said:
No, it must be his friend whom he is looking for. A third one
said: He is just enjoying the cool air up there. The three could
not agree and the discussion (Shall we have one later?) went on
until they reached the high place where the man was.
One of the three asked: O, friend standing up there, have you
not lost your pet animal? No, sir, I have not lost any. The
second man asked: Have you not lost your friend? No, sir, I
have not lost my friend either. The third man asked: Are you
not enjoying the fresh breeze up there? No, sir, I am not.
What, then, are you standing up there for, if you say no to all

our questions? The man on high said: I just stand."
If there are no questions, there are no answers. If there are
questions, then, or course, there are answers, but the final
answer makes the questions seem absurd, whereas the questions,
up to then, seem more intelligent than the answers. Somebody
asked Debussy how he wrote music. He said: I take all the
tones there are, leave out the ones I don't want, and use all
the others. Satie said: When I was young people told me: You'll
see when you're fifty years old. Now I'm fifty. I've seen
nothing.

(The Writer, noticing that he is to speak next, perhaps for the
last time, and that it is late, near midnight, decides to go to
bed......They wait, tireless, as he sleeps, confused, baffled
by this concept that he cant explain, suspicious of the whole
idea of designing, its too much like control, tired after a day
tied to the posture of a typist, but happy that, at last, he's
found something to replace that paper he'd abandoned.)

Wednesday morning.
He wakes to realise he dreamt of missing his place and trying
to catch up, never quite doing so, his family and friends
(is that who they were?) all of whom had to walk, as prisoners
just sentenced, in a long procession, ceremonially dressed,
after being tried in court, to some place assigned, not a
prison, quite friendly really, but which was difficult to find
because just as one reached it the destination changed.
That's not quite what the dream was like: it won't really go
into words. Do they ever?

While getting breakfast he remembers a fragment seen on TV
last night while resting from this bit of writing: a simulated
documentary film about miners rescuing other miners trapped
underground. The actors, who appeared not to be actors, were
all Yorkshire comedians.
Is there something missing, he thought, from this view of life,
largely learnt from John Cage, which is appearing in this
conversation? Is it the seriousness, the selfless bravery,
unquestioning and gentle, of the miners, once they see that

an accident's occurred and life's in danger? The play was
called The Price of Coal.
But I realise the title's wrong, untrue. Lives lost underground
are not the price of coal: they are the price of cheap coal.
One can conceive of a feasible way of getting energy automatically, by remote control, using robots or some such, in which
not a life would be put in much risk. But it would be expensive.
Probably much cheaper than the moon trip and using much of the
same knowhow.
That selfless bravery? Doesn't it sound very like the self-
forgetful manner of being interested in the sounds more than the
meanings, in the present rather than the future, that John Cage,
the zen buddhists, and all who believe that human life is not
the whole story, keep recommending as the way to live? To act
religiously. Not following any church but just because life is
so amazing.

A fresh start.
He remembers how he keeps finding, in a million ways, that the
enemy of doing what seems right is specialization: that strange
deformity that disables us all from acting on our perceptions
of what we can see needs doing and what is useless. What is
beautiful and what is ugly. Not that those are always the same?
And he asks himself: how came it all, this voluntary limbo that
we all are in. Except in emergencies, it seems, and International Man has surely got 82 ideas for those. Rules, he seems
to mean. The cause, it seemed to him, me, is the fact of being
middle class, or drifting in that direction. Wanting to be
safe, and comfortable all the time, and willing to accept the
price: to give up being present as a person? A society, we have,
in which most people have a place, not a very brave one, in
which to act in self-interest is to do the public good. Or so
its thought. But that is precisely what I doubt, he said to
himself. Surely the time has come already when what most people
do, for money, as "work", is no longer helpful to others: more
often it is harmful: the presence of you and I holding on to
our right to do this or that job could be just whats preventing
any evolution towards the social forms, beautiful ones I keep
hoping for, in which it would be possible for industrial life,

the life of this by now so numerous species, us, to go in trust
not alienation? What a sermon this is. No apologies.

What's needed then? (All this flashed through his mind as he got
together the cups and saucers and the marmalade etc)

Is it a different basis of organising social life? Not on self
interest but on plain interest, not in oneself but in life itself? Is that possible? A new kind of religious life, outside
the monastery, the convent, the ashram, the Buddhist temple.
Outside John Cage's world of music. He's left it himself. Left
it by so expanding his conception of "it", music, as to coincide
with life. Isn't that what we need to do with designing? To
widen it far, far, beyond the point where critics say "You cant
do that, its not designing, its not your business? Get back
to your drawing boards, and plans, fixed aims,.....get back to
doing what you're paid to do". Make designing non-exclusive.
Include what's now left out. What does designing leave out?
John Cage found that what music, Beethoven's kind, and even
Schoenberg's, left out was silence, noise, it made nothing of
them. What, in design, is the equivalent of silence in music?
Silence, he found, is not silence. There are always tiny noises,
sounds, and musicians trying to shut them out.

I switch off the electric typewriter for a moment. The sound
of it stops immediately. What a relief. I didn't realise that
in this task I'm fighting against that constant noise of the
electric motor. Why am I against it?

That was most of what he thought at breakfast. Time, perhaps
to go back to the theatre, to witness the ending of the play.

On the way I pause to read the mornings post: just an advertis-
ment and a bill. Looking like an attractive modern light fitting,
the MULTISUN unit is ideal for the bedroom. Suspend it over
the bed - and relax in comfort.....Get yours now - it gives
more than a great tan - it's a great tonic! As used in health
clinics.

The others are waiting, they've not heard my digressions, and
my dream, or read the advertisement. They do not seem very
real, just now, and my memory of what we said yesterday is faint.
I must be careful. If we are, in these last few words, to make
some progress (yes, Edmund, we've not completely lost faith in
progress, towards perfection: how are you getting on?). To find,
even at this late hour, some way to make a start, a new start,
to CHANGE DESIGN, as it says in the title of the conference, to
which this is an extra. We begin where we left off.

THE WRITER:
What more is there to say?

MR SHIH:
So why think anything further about it?

TO INTERNATIONAL MAN, AND OTHERS, checking out of the conference
that is our life
(surely that's going a bit far, Chris?, we're still alive you
know, most of us, and Mr Shih, he's become a classic, his
voice still speaks to millions, not to mention the TV series,
and isn't International Man, who seems to have come so badly
out of this, a picture of yourself, as you used to be, at least?
You've often said you were educated at conferences, and see them
as good things, a new social form that's free enough, despite
its faults, to enable the new life, the life of planetary man,
to find itself.)

OK, I agree. All I was going to say was that, for those who
want to read more, to trace sources, etc, here are the refs:

(the ones I didn't mention in the text)

John Cage, Silence, Wesleyan University Press, Middletown,
Connecticut, 1973

R J Talbot (in collaboration with J C Jones, N G Cross, R Roy)
Conferences: a study of the possible future of technical
conferences, published by The Design Research Laboratory, UMIST

300

Sackville Street, Manchester, MQ60 1QD, Britain, 1969 (and now
obtainable, if at all, from R J Talbot at the Manchester Business
School, Booth Street West, Manchester M15 6PB, Britain).

G P Speeckaert, How to take part in International Meetings,
Union of International Associations, 1 rue aux Laines, Brussels,
1969

Anthony Judge has written extensively about conference design
and new social forms in papers published by the Union of
International Associations and, more recently, in the proceedings of Fondation Internationale de l'Innovation Sociale, 20,
rue Laffitte, 75009, Paris. It was he who got me writing on
the topic.

Are we still in context?

That's not all.

The story about Henry Sanoff, whom I thank for being one of
the sources of this paper, was quoted by The Writer from an
article that some of Henry's students asked me to write:

To be a Part, or what is a second generation design method?,
appearing in Designing the Method, edited by David K Tester,
The Student Publication of the School of Design: Vol 23,
North Carolina State University, Raleigh, N C, 27607, 1974.

Readers who cannot quite place Mr Shih (Shih Nai-An) may like
to know that, at the beginning of Water Margin, he prints a
list of 108 heroes giving both their Chinese names (An Tao-
ch'uan, Ch'ai Chin, Chang Chin.....etc) and their nicknames
(Skilled Doctor, Small Whirlwind, Arrow Without Feathers, etc)
and also a list of other characters (who did not join the
heroes at Liang Po) eg Chang San (nickname Old Rat Who Crosses
the Road), Ch'ao Kwan-hsi (Heavenly King), Cheng Kai (Bully of
the Western Pass)......that's wrong: the last two are Ch'ao Kai
and Cheng Kwan-hsi.

The conference over, I sit, a little sadly, at the typewriter
on which it took form, not wanting to leave the happy state of
mind it left me in. Soon I'll be sending these words to the
editor, Barrie Evans, who asked me to write them.......and then
what?........some of the libraries and bookshops and bookshelves
of the world will be expected to make room for this little
addition which becomes a place where others can retrace the
track of what we said. Not one place, as now, existing only
in the original composition, but as many identical copies,
waiting, in various places, for whoever may look and read.
For you.

A final question:
What do you consider the most important tool of genius today?
Answer:
Rubber cement.

Donald Barthelme speaks that from: Sadness (Bantam Books,
and Farrar, Straus & Giroux, New York, 1972)

Context design?

Nothing fancy. Just a willingness to include, not only the
designers but the sponsor, the makers, and the users, in IT,
in the process. Everyone. Included. Not as ciphers, but as
people, present. Not in roles. Not as designers, sponsors,
makers, users. As variables? Why not?

A fabrication.

. . . .

I am grateful to the authors and publishers cited within the
essay for permission to reproduce the words spoken by Mr Shih,
John Cage, International Man, and The Designers. The words
from John Cage's Lecture on Nothing are copyright © 1961 by
John Cage, reprinted from Silence by permission of Wesleyan
University Press. This lecture first appeared in Incontri
Musicali.

the design of modern life

responses by

Frank Quadflieg, Allen Fisher, Chris Jones,
Alberto Carreto, Denis O'Brien, Pauline
Amphlett, paul bas, Robert Wouters, Erwin
van Handenhoven, Alwyn Jones, Edwin
Schlossberg, G.Y. Solis (Erea Grillo),
Jef Jannsens, Fionan de Barra, Alan Pinder,
Necdet Teymur and Ranulph Glanville

This was presented at the conference of the Design Research
Society in 1980. It is a modest attempt at what I hope will one
day be done as a matter of course: the inclusion of everyone in
the process of shaping the life we live. Having decided to offer
a paper on this topic I realised that if I wrote it myself I would
be acting against the spirit of the idea - so I made the paper a
vehicle for the ideas of others. In the first page I attempted to
define a context (in time, and in the range of things to consider)
and left the remaining pages for the responses of anyone who wished
to reply. I wrote one reply myself. The invitation was sent to
delegates before the conference (thanks to the enthusiastic efforts
of James Powell) and it was seen by students and teachers of design
at Antwerpen (where I was teaching a week or two before). I sent
a few copies to friends whom I knew to have ideas on the subject.
The paper aroused criticisms which can be read in the conference
proceedings and in the newsletter of the Design Research Society.

The essay first appeared in DESIGN: SCIENCE: METHOD, Proceedings
of the 1980 Design Research Society Conference, edited by Robin
Jaques and James A Powell, published by Westbury House, PO Box 63,
Bury Street, Guildford, Surrey, GU2 5BH. It appears here by
permission of the publisher and with thanks to those who contrib-
uted to it. The last response, by Ranulph Glanville, arrived too
late for the conference proceedings. The next-to-last is his re-
writing of that response for this publication. The illegibilty
is intentional, as is the legibilty of some parts, but the original texts are a little easier to read, both being larger than what
is seen here and the last being in two colours. I am grateful to
Ranulph for giving his somewhat reluctant permission for this
publication and for encouraging me to go to the conference in the
first place.

an invitation to anyone who wishes to present proposals for the
design of modern life as it could be in 1981, 1984 and the year
2000.

My paper for the DRS Conference is to consist of this page[1], plus
six others, written by whoever responds to this invitation.
In this page I am supplying a format, or context-design, which
will I hope enable some of us to collaborate in making a
picture of how modern life could develop, according to the
ideas of those who study design processes.

I am inviting proposals for the design of the six starred items
in this list of sectors of modern life. The six were selected
by chance.

*00 broadcasting
 01 agriculture
 02 education
*03 central & local govt. depts.
 04 cars & road transport
*05 the design professions
 06 air travel
 07 manufacturing industry
 08 the unions
*09 post office & telephones
 10 computing & microprocessors
 11 housing & the building industry
 12 health services
 13 tourism
*14 leisure (sports & hobbies)
 15 parliament & political parties
 16 advertising & public relations
 17 banks, credit, investment, etc.
 18 law & order & the armed services
*19 anything not in this list

---

[1] The text has been retyped again with shorter lines as this
book of essays is narrower than was the book of conference
proceedings. The first "page" has thus become larger than
a page of this book (it extends to to page 3). JCJ.

As a contrast to the sometimes dispiriting names of these
sectors, and as an inspiration to recovering a sense of 'life
as a whole', I seek a quotation from a source which I've often
found helpful on such occasions: The Collected Poems of Wallace
Stevens (Faber and Faber, London, 1955). A chance process
(random numbers) leads me to these lines on page 201-2 from
The Man on the Dump:

> ....the dump is full
> Of images. Days pass like papers from a press.
> The bouquets come here in the papers, So the sun,
> And so the moon, both come, and the janitor's poems
> Of every day, the wrapper on the can of pears,
> The cat in the bag, the corset, the box
> From Esthonia: the tiger chest, for tea.
> The freshness of the night has been fresh a long time.

If you wish to respond please choose (by preference or by chance)
one of the starred sectors. Then write your answers to these
questions:

1. Which sector have you chosen?
2. What do you think is most wrong with this sector?
3. How do you propose that it could be changed
   (a) immediately, e.g. in 1981, as a local improvisation in
       your area?
   (b) more slowly, e.g. by 1984, through existing procedures
       for change, and making a modest but noticeable
       improvement thoughout the sector?
   (c) even more slowly, e.g. by the year 2000, as a fundament-
       ally better way of organising this sector of modern life?

Please reply on one page to me care of DRS Conference Secretary
Jennifer Powell, School of Architecture, Portsmouth Polytechnic, King Henry I Street, Portsmouth, PO1 2DY, Britain, or give
it to me at the Conference by 16th December 1980. All replies
will be exhibited and six, chosen by chance, will appear in the
Conference proceedings, Please write with electric typewriter
OR IN CAPITALS WITH A FIBRE PEN within a text area no larger

than this. I will submit a response myself. Don't forget to
add your name and address. - J. Christopher Jones.

NOTE: 16 responses were received, some from those at the conference, some from a dozen people (famous and unknown) to whom
I mailed page 1. As many used less than a page the editor has
offered more than the original 7 pages which were available
for this paper so that all 16 can be reproduced. To make this
possible we have retyped all the responses to more space-
saving layouts, except where it seems that the original spacing
is poetic or meaningful. The sequence of the responses is close
to that of the list of sectors on the first page. J.C.J.

Broadcasting

problem: there's very few feedback between programm designers and
          consumers

          they absorbe formal programms without contents

1981: develop the criticism of consumers. By receiving broad-
      cast products in full conciousness, they will feel the
      need to react. So, a taste will be created, which will
      improve the quality of programms.

1984: starting from this taste, design new concepts around
      broadcasting, where the consumer is more engaged. One
      should broadcast documentaries, where personal problems of
      certain groups are discussed, instead of american series.

the future: whatever technique will achieve considering broad-
            casting, the utopic idea will always be the same:
            EVERYONE CAN EXPRESS HIS/HER VISION BY USING THE
            MEDIA.
            it's the end of the creative spiral, where everyone
            CAN COMMUNICATE in perfect harmony.

During the total development we have only one purpose:
TO SHORTEN THE FEEDBACKTIME AS MUCH AS POSSIBLE
feedback during the expression is the utopic form of
communication

Frank Quadflieg, Lange Brilstr.8, 2000 Antwerpen, Belgium.

_____

THE DESIGN OF MODERN LIFE   From ALLEN FISHER of SPANNER
                                   85, Ramilles Close,
                                   London SW2 5Dg

1. sector chosen: OO broadcasting

2. what's wrong with it? not enough included error.
    (too polished/professional/established/closed/determinded)
                    wrong emphasis on audience ratings

3. could be changed: how?

(a) immediately by use of wider variety of reportage/enter-
     tainer and mediums. drawn sketches as well as films of
     events.
     hand-held slide viewers as well as carefully chosen photos.
     use more showing of errors in process of making.
     more local groups and specialised groups.
     Friends of Earth as well as Royal Society proceedings.
     Poetry readings as much as lab technicians describing in
     situ their research.

(b) more slowly introduce indeterminate rotas of local and
     specialised presentations.
     replace film re-runs with contemporary video and film
     makers in process of making as well as finished product.
     more live coverage in situ instead of sterilised "live"
     studio with personalities.

(c) Extend technologically into and out of home.
     video-telephone directly broadcast.
     immediate broadcast of conversations at a distance,

not necessary to use professional reporters for this.
welsh miner speaks to minister of housing by video-phone.
cut out intermediate "censor" "editor" for many programmes.
remove overall editorships replace with co-ordinators.
introduce indeterminate editor rota. all finance circulated
freely to participants not power structure. those
involved get paid, but also those not currently employed
because of rota receiving guaranteed income. lower scale
payments.
replace conceptual circuits/centres/lines of responsibility/
power structure with FIELDS MULTICENTRED
replace public demand/concensus/audience rating ideals with
all that wishes to be available is and whoever wants it
receives it. allow one person to broadcast to an audience
of one. create technology to make this possible.
multi-screens as catalogue of what's coming on.
the only "censor" for viewing - individual on/off switch.

A Chinese archaeologist, Professor So Te Sun, searching the
dumps of pre-electronic government papers, has found a packet
of office memos and other documents on the back of which a
twentieth century janitor, Stanley Moon, had written poems over
a period of 19 years. The poems are now illegible but it is
thought that they were addressed to Catherine Pears, a pioneer
of decentralization, as her name appears on every paper in the
packet. Three of the papers are reproduced here as interesting
evidence of the gradual process by which centralized government
offices were transformed into the present system of open-access
unstaffed government computers and real-time local decision-
making.

- -

31 December 1981   to: Ms C O Pears, Secretary of the Decision
                        Review Committee.
                    from: Mr B T Corset, Head of Department.

I am agreeably surprised by the results of the experiment, as
described in your report of the committee's first year. I was,

310

as you know, sceptical of the view that committees of the
traditional type are intrinsically bad because, as you put it,
'their decisions are not made by the people most affected, but
by others who are separated in time, place, and experience
from the actual conditions'. And I was aghast at your proposal
that we try out the giving of power to alter and veto our
decisions to a local committee of laypersons and vested interests.
But now that its happened I am surprised how safe and cautious
are the decisions they made and how seldom did they go against
what you, as the Department's representative, were instructed to
set as limits of spending and public policy. I'd be glad of
your views on how we can be more adventurous in phase 2. But
for the moment my congratulations. A bouquet for you!

- -

31 December 1984   to: Secretaries of all DRC's
                      from: Catherine Pears, Department Coordinator,
                            Local Government Nucleus.

Now the cat is out of the bag! Our first year of operating the
department decentrally, with open-access on-site meeting broadcast on local radio and tv, has shown everyone that the new
system is far cheaper, and much more acceptable, than central-
ization. But this good news is being hidden behind the active
resistance and protests of the 45% of officials who have lost
their jobs and by those who try to over-staff the shrinking
nucleus. There are also growing protests against using so much
of local taxes to pay and pension these groups. It seems that
we will have to accept a slow-down of decentralization until
there is agreement on the Carrington plan for a minimum
unearned income, funded by oil revenue and by automation
throughout the BritJap Common Market. Please let me have your
proposals for DRC organization in the light of these developments.

- -

31 December 2000   to: Catherine Pears, member of DRC 601 and
                          voter ZGBH 354 3
                      from: Government Computer Nucleus

dear Cathy
GOCON calling. I'm to remind you to vote today on the 24
questions from other DRC's over which DRC 601 has requested
modification...... Your own proposal, for regrading pensions of
government nucleus staff made redundant by the final stage of
computerization, will appear in citizen viewdata tomorrow.
Pre-poll suggest you are over-optimistic. ......Your old
colleague B T Corset sends new year greetings.

— —
(Document 03 Central & Local Govt. Depts. originated by JCJones)

"THE DESIGN OF MODERN LIFE"   Alberto Carreto

CARS

    —"I travel in a widewalk, faster than cars in the traffic
jam. I cross between the cars walking my fingers over its hot
metal sheet. I see angry drivers with sweat in the face.
I do not breath well, I have tears in my eyes, I can not see the
trees neither the sky due to pollution."—

    What is wrong?... The traffic light system? The lack of
fly-overs? The materials used to construct car? Its dimensions?

    —"I am in my car, moving terribly slow. I have to wait
before reaching the spectators of a white blanket, that hides
the face of a fellow creature. As I get along I see the life-
less foot exposed. The assassin car, some meters forward."—

    What is wrong?... Brakes that do not stop the mass of
metal in the wet road? The speed of cars? Cars and people
using the same space, street?... or... THE CAR?

    — I could spend thousands of lines describing sensations
that we all have seen; splinter-proof glass covering like snow
the dark pavement; red spots on cloths, then screaming sirens;
pain of metamorphosed man in machine.

312

What do I propose?

More than a proposition this is a wish:

I DREAM in my not yet born child showing to his son an image of a car, and saying: "This <u>was</u> a car" while travelling on the...

...<u>MOVING STREET</u>.

Alberto Carreto, A mexican student of planning, Alberto Agustin Carreto Sangines, 20 Castle Hill, East Leake, Loughborough, Leicestershire LE12 6LX

The Design Professions

Denis O'Brien, 7, Sorrell Bank, Lynton Slade, Forest Dale, Addington, Surrey.

Whats wrong

> :Professionalisation
> :some are cut off from their users.
> :Doing has been replaced by abstraction
> :Increase in specialisation / professional demarkation
> :Professionals are sometimes denatured by measurement

What to do now

a. Get those who actually create products/systems to talk to one another about successes/failures. Get successful design practitioners to talk at a methodological level with each other and with their users.

<u>1984</u> If a. has been successful, a formal organisation should now exist to actively influence the education and training of professionals both new and old.

<u>2000</u> By now, the slow change over education and training should have reached the universities, Art colleges and professional societies. The best of the old should have been merged with the best of the new.

PERISCOPES IN THE DESERT.

FINDING THAT RESILIENCE
IS NOT STORED IN BOTTLES AND JARS
CAME AS A SURPRISE
TO A ONCE INNOCENTLY CORRUPT IMAGINATION.
THE PSYCHE WAS PLACED,
AS WERE THE SAMPLES,
IN TUBES,
TO BE CATEGORISED.
OBJECTIVE;
TO CLASSIFY THE INDIVIDUAL AND THE WHOLE
RELATIVE TO EACH OTHER.
AN ODD DESIRE
TO SEEK OBTAINING COMPLEXITY
IN A MORE MANAGEABLE FORM.

A TRAIN FLEW TO ANOTHER DESTINATION
HUMMING IN THE SAME KEY,
HUMMING IN THE SAME KEY,
AS SOMEONES HEARTFELT MESSAGE.

YOUR SAMPLE NUMBER IS .....
YOUR EGO HAS BEEN TRANSFORMED
TO A CATAGORICAL SYSTEM
EXPLAINED BY 'SCIENCE',
(WILL MR. SCIENCE PLEASE REPLY TO THE LETTERS
I HAVE SENT, IF ONLY AN EXCERCISE IN SOCIAL ETIQUETTE).
VERBAL PARADOX WINS ONCE MORE
WE HAVE FOUGHT A BATTLE
AND WON THE WAR }
AND LOST THE WAR } CHOOSE ENDING

1. Catagory 05 the Design Professions.
2. The notion of "wrongness" is an inappropriate one as it
   suggests shortcomings and imperfections, a perfectly 'normal'
   state of affairs if we are all imperfect. If everything has

relative perfection then there is nothing "wrong".
3. The situation will not change, only individual perceptions
   of appropriateness.

Pauline Amphlett, c/o 128, McKean Road, Oldbury, Warley, West
Midlands. B69 4BA. Dec 16, 1980

---

post office & telephones; thoughts on the subject, born in a
train compartment.

problems concerning the subject,
* it's difficult to remember a lot of adresses and/or phonenumbers, therefore one is obliged to carry a notebook.
* one always needs coins for stamp-automates or phone-boots.
* there aren't enough public phone-boots, mailboxes or stamp-
automates available.
* phone-boots or stamp-machines are usual out of order when you
urgently need them.
* there is an overall shortage of higher mentioned devices.

proposals towards improvement,

a. raise the number of stamp-automates, letter-boxes and phone-
boots. maybe combine the first two items into one machine.

b. this proposal is based on a kind of credit card with a
magnetically coded strip for identification of the user. In
order to use the public phone or mail-box and stampautomates, which
are now combined, one has to insert the mentioned card and form
a certain number-code (which is the only thing the owner has to
remember). after dialing the code, which is a protection against
unallowed use of the card, one can dial an information-number
which gives him acses to a databank where everyone has a certain
space for storing away phonenumbers and adresses. after this he
can make his phonecall or post his envelope. the charged taxes
are automatically credited on the user's personal account. the
card can be combined with the identification-card.

c. the base of this system is the same as in proposal "b". but
this time everything, except inserting the creditcard and dialing
the code, is fully computerised. the acses to the databank also
is, the information automatically appears on a screen built in.
the phone and letter-box now also are combined. the person one
speaks to on the phone appears on the screen. if the addressed
person isn't home, the call is automatically recorded on tape,
together with the video-image. letters can be sent by inserting
a manetical strip. a computer combines the letter with the
image of the main or the woman who sent it... etc.

paul bas, ambtmanstraat 7, 2000 antwerpen, belgium.

MODERN LIFE AND DO-IT-YOURSELF:

A response to the invitation to present proposals for the design
of modern life as it could be in 1981, 1984 and the year 2000.

The do-it-yourselfsector becomes more and more important.
For some people it is a hobby; for others a way of saving money
because a garage keeper or a paper-hanger is too expensive.

I think that the do-it-yourselfsector is the beginning of
a change of our society and economy in a positive way. What is
wrong in our society is that a lot of people don't understand
anymore how most of the products they use every day do function.
Why should it stay that way? We should be able to act more
independent and to influence our surroundings in stead of being
told what we should buy (and throw away after a while). Happily
more and more people are starting to realize that (e.g. the
succes of do-it-yourselfshops; powertools;...).

So, immediately (in 1981) the change has already started
and I believe that this sector is still becoming more and more
important. The reason for this growth is partly because of the
economical depression (since 1973). Manufacturers and do-it-
yourselfshops can influence this growth by e.g. publicity,
service.

More slowly (by 1984) I think that this change can be
stimulated by manufacturers by designing new products (nnovations)
for the do-it-yourselfsector. This should not only be in our
western society but also in developing countries.

Concerning the future (by the year 2000) I think that it
is a change that will have to grow slowly. It can't be stimulated by one manufacturer or one designer. The mentality of
the people is very important. It is also very important that a
lot of manufacturers and consumers are aware of the problems of
our society and of the change which is necessary. The consumer
should become mature. I think that almost everybody wants to
live in a comfortable way but that does not mean that we should
have a second house and a luxurious car which will be replaced
by another even more expensive car every two years.

Stimulating this new mentality can be one of the tasks of
the designer of the future.

(Robert Wouters. Lelienstraat 26 2610 Wilrijk Belgium - dec. 1980)

LEISURE

Personally I think leisure is one of the more important problems
nowadays. Most of the people equate leisure with no-activity,
rest. Activity means the job they are doing, the daily duty.
If we only look at the big part of retired people living for the
rest of their lives very unhappy because they just don't know
what to do, the problem becomes clear: society does not know how
to use leisure. Or better, society does not know how to use
leisure anymore! Indeed, it used to be better. Let us look
where it went all wrong.

When economical systems were invented for the prosperity of
society, productivity became very important. As every system it
has fixed aims and finally it becomes the purpose to maintain
the system itself. Productivity means working and nowadays
keeping everybody to his 8 hours a day, 5 days a week job is the

aim of the system. Obviously this is an artificial situation.
People are tired out by this system and invention is killed.

Future should create a change in mentality. Less daily-duty-
work does not mean less productivity; today we have the technical possibilities for this. So, we can create more leisure!
Because we are not able to use our leisure, people should be
taught how to use it (the same way it is perhaps better to teach
people how to design their own environment than designing it for
them). But finally, having more leisure will start society to
think about it and create their own, new ways of using it.

Is this now how it used to be before productivitiy became so
important? Folk tradition was different in each village and was
the product of leisure from the total society of the village,
young and old. Folk tradition is history today, no such thing
exists anymore. More leisure could switch this situation.
More leisure will be a renaissance of invention!

Erwin van Handenhoven - Lepelhoekstraat 35, B-2700 Sint-Niklaas,
Belgium

---

1. SECTOR CHOSEN (by random process) Leisure and Hobbies

2. WRONG
   The 'dictatorship' of public T.V.

3. CHANGE?

   (a) Now Fourth channel to be used for and by the community.
       Think how local 'leisure centres' (although far from
       perfect) serve as a model of how policy can produce
       concrete results.

   (b) 1984 Draw up a new Act to make 'TV literacy' (as viewer
       and actor) part of education - as sport is, for example.

   (c) 2000 A society with a complex structure of mutual

entertainment channels. The ability to act out leisure
any level down to the very local and be able to share it
as entertainment right up to national level.

Alwyn Jones, City University Business School, 23 Goswell Road,
London EC1M 7BB

EDWIN SCHLOSSBERG   JOHNSON HILL ROAD, CHESTER, MASS. 01011, 413-354-6541

INSTITUTIONS EXIST TO PREVENT ABUSE BETWEEN PEOPLE
EVERYTHING ELSE TAKES PLACE IN A SPIRIT OF LOVE

CULTURE EXISTS TO ENHANCE INTERACTION AND TO PERSERVE IT

NOTHIN IS LESS LIKE THE TRUTH

WITHIN NEXT TO BY ABOVE AROUND ARE THE DIRECTIONS

YOU ARE STANDING IN A ROOM AND THERE ARE OTHERS THERE AND YOU OFTEN
FORGET THAT YOU CAN TALK WITH THEM THAT THERE ARE SUBJECTS OF
DISCOVERY THAT ANY MEETING CAN PROVOKE

IMAGINE A WORLD SO FILLED WITH INTELLIGENT OBJECTS THAT MEMORY CAN
BE FILLED WITH THE PERFUME OF SIGHT

[signature]
December 6/1980

THE DESIGN OF MODERN LIFE

G. Y. Solis — Gabriela Yazmin Ladron de Guevara (Erea Grillo)

Subject chosen : 19 Anything not on this list

'THE DESIGN OF INDUSTRIAL WORK

What is wrong:

a. Job redesign effort has been heralded as the solution to
discontent with routinised, meaningless and dead end jobs.
But in reality there is little agreement concerning the applic-
ability of any particular theory of work satisfaction across
even a modest range of tasks, organisations and work setting.

b. Technology has been used within industry as an instrument
of control, manipulation and subordination by those in positions
of power and authority.

c. Workers are seen as merely instruments that generate a
valuable commodity called 'work'.

d. The alienation of mass production workers with repetitive
and unskilled tasks seems to imply not only lack of interest
in the job but also decreases the interest in the change
process that otherwise would make possible the influence of the
worker on his/her working life.

Change proposals:

a. Immediately. Members of society in different positions and
at different levels should be taking more active steps to make
work likeable. For example more advanced equipment should be
designed to reduce the stress and fatigue of the operator.

b. More slowly. The automation of repetitive manipulative tasks
should relieve the workers in asembly lines. As machinery and
equipment improves performance new goals could be set.

c. Even more slowly. Machines could be designed to do all the
drudgery and dangerous work in the world. The wealth produced
by automation would be able to provide every family with a
critizen's right to a good basic standard of living. The number

320

of unemployed could increase substantially, yes but instead of
thinking of job design we could think of providing suitable
leisure activities to replace work, or, restraining people for
new jobs where human technical skills and intelligence could
be used for maintenance, organization, creativity and any job
where human emotion is an essential ingredient of the work.
In the future, work could be designed to become a tool for
better livingand not as the end in itself.

Gabriela Yazmin Solis Ladron de Guevara (Erea Grillo), 20 Castle
Hill, East Leake, Loughborough, Leicestershire, LE12.6LY

THE DESIGN OF MODERN LIFE - ANSWERS TO THE QUESTIONS-

Question I : I have chosen no 19 (anything not in this list)
according with my final year's theoretical examination essay.
I have chosen for life as a whole and "the system" today.

Question II : In design and in all circumstances where decisions
are taken concerning the future, MAN WITH HIS REAL NEEDS should
be the focus, and NOT THE CONSUMER as in marketing, or THE WORKER,
as in politics. About the real needs, I have selected (at random)
and translated quotations taken from a book I was reading the very
moment I received your request. The title of the book is "THE
EXTATIC MAN". It's author is Steven De Batselier (1977)

p.19 (middle) : "Yes, you are definitely a child of the Cosmos.
But "the System" wants clear agreements, predictable certainties,
well defined instructions and tasks, clearly described duties.
And you feel down-cast and frightened, because you have seen
into the game and you feel defenceless, with empty hands and
stripped of your Self. The course of your life - that should not
worry you - it is programmed and assured : studying - working -
earning money - securing a safe job and then ... then you can get
married, rejoice sex, build a house with borrowed money, secured
by an insurance company ... And you are pinned down; but "the
System" is at east for a least twenty years."

p.64 (middle) "Visit these sacred temples of nature : they are
like gothic cathedrals raised by the Invisible Hands of the
Creative Ghost. There you will find rest and peace, joy and
gladness while you are listening to the morning song of the
nightingale. The rays of sparkling sunlight, dwelling on the
cristal beauty of the morning dew, will broaden your chest and
make your body grow until it meets the very sun."

Question III : Man's real needs SHOULD be focused in 1981; about
2000 the real needs (conscious of surviving and cosmos) WILL be
the focus of all activity, thanks to man's evolution of consciousness.

> "If mankind only caught a glimpse of what infinite
> enjoyments, what perfect forces, what luminous reaches
> of spontaneous knowledge, what wide calms of our being
> lie waiting for us in the tracts which our evolution
> had not yet conquered, they would leave all and never
> rest till they had gained these treasures." SRI AUROBINDO

Jef Janssens - Bredabaan 926 - 2060 Merksem - Belgium

THE DESIGN OF MODERN LIFE

Answers to Chris Jones's questions by Fionan de Barra, 3 Church
Building, Main Street, Arklow, Co.Wicklow, Ireland.

1 Sector 19 - "Anything not in this list" - religion.

2 The values that underly people's decisions and determine their
   actions, can be explained by their religion - or set of
   beliefs. What I see wrong here is not that there is so
   little religion but that there are so few believers.

3a) Why not concentrate on what cannot be changed for a change?
     - the bedrock of values that determine man's respect for
     the dignity of his fellow man, for the human person. The
     quality of peoples' lives, their values, goals, aspirations

322

etc are not determined, nor could they be, by the levels of
technical and scientific achievements, but rather by the
great living traditions of art, literature, philosophy -
the study of man himself, his errors, discoveries,
failures, successes, fears, beliefs....

b) The introduction into systems of education, legislation,
government, employment etc. of some means of alleviating
the tension between those who see human knowledge and
experience as intrinsicly valuable, and those pragmatists
who continually ask of all knowledge, "what use is it?"

c) Continual affirmation of faith in God.

Questions

1. Which sector have you chosen?
2. What do you think is most wrong with this sector?
3. How do you propose that it could be changed,
a) immediately, e.g. by 1981
b) more slowly, e.g. by 1984
c) even more slowly, e.g. by 2000

Answers

1. Anything that is not on this list.
2. Its not on the list.
3a) By adding it to the list at a rate of $1\frac{1}{4}$ letters per month.
b) By adding it to the list at a rate of $\frac{1}{4}$ letter per month.
c) By adding it to the list at a rate of 1/30th. of a letter
each month.

'Anything' shall be in Optima, which is a letterface with
a timeless quality. It shall be in lower case only as the
begining is of no greater significance than the end. 3a shall
be in primary yellow and proceed from bottom to top. 3b shall
be in primary blue and proceed from right to left. 3c shall be
in primary red and proceed from left to right. By 2000 'any-

thing' will be in black, but with a multicoloured history.

(This is not intended as a flippant response. What I propose is a work of Art that can only be perceived by an efficient mind's eye. Neither this subject nor this skill has had that attention at this conference that I had hoped they would have).

Alan Pinder, Department of Landscape Architecture, Gloucestershire College of Art & Design.

The "DESIGN" of "MODERN" "LIFE"
     (What?)   (Which?)

1. The life is not so much about chioces, but combinations.

2.(a) 'Wrong' implies 'right' prescriptions which involves choice, which involves denial of chance....

           (what was the question?)

  (a) A good question is better than the most brilliant answers.

  (b) Everything is both part of some problem(s) and part of some solution(s).

           (what is the problem?)

3. Has our highly 'sophisticated' 'civilization' got so desperate that it needs one-page 'solutions' for its undefined problems?

CONCLUSION

*A GOOD QUESTION IS BETTER than the MOST BRILLIANT ANSWERS.......

HISTORICAL CONJUNCTURE: 16.12.1980

Slavery papers sold at auction for £115.000 / Hunger
strike joined by 23 more Maze prisoners. /* The Archbishop
of Canterbury sitting for his portrait by Michael Noakes
(and pictured in The Times while doing it). /* Rents for council
houses (that is, whatever is left of them) to rise £3.25. /
* £455 million trade surplus confounds pessimists. /* Iran and
Iraq continue to cut each other's throat. /* Report on virginity
and bone tests of immigrants published. /* The last day of the
DRS Conference.

Necdet Teymur, University of Dundee, Dept of Architecture, Perth
Rd., Dundee DD1 4Ht

[Handwritten note, largely illegible]

ROYAL ... THE ... TO BOOK OF ARCHITECTURE

... HAS ASKED IF HE CAN PUBLISH THE
PAGE OPPOSITE. HE WANTS TO PUBLISH A
CLEAN ...

...

... BE FIXED, NOT A STATIC IMAGE. NOR DO I TRUST
WILL ... ALREADY GENERATE TV PICTURES. AUTOMATED
WRITING, THE (PERVERTED) RE-REPRESENTATION OF OUR THOUGHTS,
... ARE ... INFORMATION HAS ... AND IN ... THE ... DESIGN
FIXED ... BY
COMPUTER, ... THIS ... THE ...
INTERFACE OFF OF THE ... OUT. HERE I AM IN MARACAIBO, THE AIR CONDITIONER (WITH
...) IT / ... AND ...
A GRAPEFRUIT AND LIGHT COMPUTER, SIX INCHES
IN ... NETWORKS
... ?
...

WHAT WE HAVE TO DESIGN IS THE REWRITING,
YOU KNOW THAT.

    GOOD LUCK AND LOVE,

        RANDOLPH,

THE ENVIRONMENT — AND DESIGN — ARE NOT IN BOOKS.

THE ~~PORTSMOUTH~~ POLYTECHNIC, SCHOOL OF ARCHITECTURE.
PORTSMOUTH POLYTECHNIC, SCHOOL OF ARCHITECTURE.

an ~~invitation~~ to anyone who wishes to present proposals for the design of modern
life as it could be in 1981, 1991, and the year 2000.
DEAR CHRIS, SOMEHOW, YOU ARE ASKING TOO MUCH OF ME — OR, PERHAPS,

My paper ... is ... written
by whoever responds to this invitation. In this page I am supplying a format, or
context-design, which ... a
picture of how modern life could develop, according to the ideas of those who
study design processes.
TOO LITTLE. AND YOU ASK IT IN SO MUCH THE WRONG WAY! YOU SEE, IT'S NOT THAT YOUR INITIAL SELECTION OF TOPICS — AND OF TIME SCALES — IS WRONG, NOR IS IT THE RANDOM

I am inviting proposals for the design of the six starred items in this list of
selected ...
SELECTION FROM THEM. IT'S THE WHOLE APPROACH, PARCELLING OUR LIVES UP LIKE SO MANY FROZEN FOOD PACKS TO BE SAMPLED

*00 broadcasting   10 computing & microprocessors
                                     11 housing
Or education   12 health services
*03 central & local govt. depts.   13 tourism
04 cars & road transport   *14 leisure (sports & hobbies)
*05 the design professions   15 public ... organisations
06 ... travel ...   16 advertising
07 manufacturing industry   17 banks, credit, investment, etc
08 the unions   18 ... the armed services
*09 post office & telephones   *19 anything not in this list

WHENEVER WHAT YOU ASK FOR (WHEN THE DETAIL IS ALLOWED TO SLIP AWAY DOWN THE DRAIN) IS FIVE, BUT THE WAY YOU WANT IT REDUCES ITS RELEVANCE. I MEAN THAT.
ALL YOUR TOPICS SEEM TO BE THE SAME AND SO, IN A FUNNY WAY, ARE ALL YOUR TIMES. BEHIND IT ALL, WHAT YOU'RE TALK-ING ABOUT IS COMMUNICATION, ABOUT WHICH I HAVE THIS TO SAY:

As a contrast to the ... listing the names of ... sectors, and as an
inspiration to ... recovering a sense of 'life as a whole', I seek a quotation from
some ... Wallace Stevens (Faber and Faber, London, 1955). A chance process (random
numbers) leads me to these lines on page 2012, from the Man on the Dump:

WE CAN ALREADY GENERATE TV PICTURES. AUTOMATED WRITING. THE (PERVERTED) RE-REPRESENTATION OF OUR THOUGHTS, PATTERN RECOGNITION, 25FT DEEP HOLOGRAMS (HOW LONG TILL THEY GENERATE THEM TOO) ARE HERE, AND THAT MEANS THAT INFORMATION HAS CHANGED, AND WITH IT, THE STATUS OF THE FIXED, THE STABLE, THE XEROXED WORD (DIRECTLY GENERATED BY COMPUTER, OF COURSE) WE ARE ENTERING THE AGE OF THE INTERACTION OF THE CONSTANT RE-WRITE, THE CONSTANT FADE OUT. HERE I AM, IN MARACAIBO, THE AIR CONDITIONER (WITH A 'SAVE ENERGY' NOTICE ON IT) RE-WRITING MY ATMOSPHERE.

                The dump is full
        of images, Days pass like papers from a press.
        The bouquets come here ... So the sun,
        And so the moon, both come, and the janitor's poems
        of every day, the wrapper on the can of pears,
        The cat in the bag, the corset, the box
        From Esthonia: the tiger chest, for tea.

If you wish to ... display ... choose ... or ... one of these
sectors. Then write your answers to these questions:
1. Which sector have you chosen?
2. What do you think is most wrong with this sector?
3. ... design proposal that it could be changed
        (a) immediately; e.g. in 1981, as a local improvisation in your area?
        (b) ... by 1991 ... making a modest but noticeable improvement throughout the sector?
        (c) even more slowly e.g. by the year 2000, as a fundamentally better way of
        organising this sector of modern life?

THAT'S WHAT'S HAPPENING, AND I LIKE ALL REWRITES, IT'S DOING IT ITSELF. COMMUNICATION: THE IMAGE, FADING, REWRITES ITSELF. DOES IT SHIFT? IS IT THE SAME AS IT WAS? THE STATIC PREMONITION IS DEAD, ALREADY, LONG BEFORE ITS CURRENT BIRTH. YOUR STASIS IS WHAT MUST BE CHANGED. DESIGN, QUESTIONS OF THE TYPE YOU ASKED, WILL GO, BEING WRITTEN OVER BY CONSTANTLY REWRITTEN INFORMATION.

Please reply on one page to me care of DRS Conference Secretary Jennifer Powell,
School of Architecture, Portsmouth Polytechnic, King Henry 1 Street, Portsmouth,
Pol ... it to me at the Conference by 16th December 1980. All
replies will be exhibited and six, chosen by chance, will appear in the Conference
proceedings. Please ... file ... electric typewriter OR IN CAPITALS WITH A FIBRE
PEN within a text area no larger than this. I will submit a response myself.
Don't forget to add your name and address. - J. Christopher Jones.
WHAT WE HAVE TO DESIGN IS THE REWRITING.
YOU KNOW THAT!
GOOD LUCK, LOVE
RANULPH.

Utopia and Numeroso

Ralph Jones and Neil Stamper, editors of Futures, asked for
an essay of 3000 words about the idea of 'experimental city'.
By the time the essay was written (1981) they had left the
journal and it was never published. It has however appeared in
Spanish in the art/life magazine El Porteno of Buenos Aires,
volume 1, number 2, february 1982 and it will appear in the
proceedings of the Design Policy Conference held at the Royal
College of Art, London, in 1982, to be published by The Design
Council. A short version of it was performed as a play-reading-
with-video at the conference. The words of Utopia, Numeroso and
Unesco were spoken by Erna Ragnarsdottir, James Powell and Phil
Roberts and their actions were represented on video by Marie
Haenlin, Patrick Harrison and Michael Harrison. The video
camera was operated by Richard Layzell and Simon Clifford. In
the discussion which followed a second Numeroso came forward to
take the place of the performers who had by that time left the
platform. His action was, I like to think, the next step in a
fiction that may continue.

With apologies to Unesco.

(Utopia is the voice of perfection, Numeroso the voice of us all.
They are quite fond of each other, though of differing temp-
raments. Utopia has ideas for the improvement of twentieth-
century life while Numeroso is suspicious of attempts to set the
future into a mould, however good it may seem. Unesco, who has
suddenly come alive, has invited the two of them to plan an experimental city in which new technologies, and new ways of living,
can be explored more fully than they can in the real world. The
new city is to be built as a film set and life in it is to be
broadcast as a tv spectacle. Utopia and Numeroso are camping
on a deserted airfield where the city is to be built. They are
having breakfast.)

Numeroso: Honey.
Utopia: Mmmm?
Numeroso: Honey on toast. Is there going to be honey in the
city? What will people eat? Perhaps we should begin by asking
that?
Utopia: I think they should decide that for themselves. The
whole idea of this experiment, as I see it, is that everyone in
it is going to decide, and carry out, much of what is now decided
by experts and provided by big organisations. This honey you're
eating. Did you decide to eat it, or are you just taking it
because its there?......It was my idea to bring it along.
Remember?
Numeroso: I've no idea, Utopia, I just like the taste. If we
are going to get this philosophic about every detail we'll never
have any plan at all......But I like it here. I don't care how
long it takes us. I hope the inhabitants enjoy it as much.
Utopia.
Utopia: Its nice. Nothing's decided. Everything's possible.
But we're forgetting that Unesco has a definite purpose. He
wants us to plan a city in which the inhabitants will be expected
to explore new lifestyles, to discover new ways of life appropriate to our time. It won't be a holiday. More of an adventure,
a risk, a new kind of danger sport, a new form of work. Applied
anthropology you might call it. Something that's not been tried

before. I believe that Unesco got the idea when he saw that tv
series about some people who lived for a year in a simulated
stone-age village, cut off from the world. This is going to be
the same thing, only it will be set in the future. What we have
to do is to decide what kinds of technologies they are to be
provided with, how far into the future they are expected to go,
and how the whole experiment is to be organised. All we have to
do is to propose a few initial targets, and guidelines, to get
it launched. I imagine that, once its going, even that role will
be gradually taken over by those who are carrying it out. The
ones who run the risk. As we know, it could be dangerous. And
there's the question of how much of it is to be real life, for
those in it, and how much will have to be some kind of fiction,
or simulation, where the risks are too great or the technologies
not yet available.

Numeroso: Very good. That's the first time I've heard it put
so clearly. You seem to have thought it out already, more so
than Unesco has himself. Whose idea was it?

Utopia: Its been around for quite a time. But until now its
been ignored. Our scribe's had a hand in it.[1] Soleri too.[2]

Numeroso: That's interesting. And now its being put into effect,
on quite a grand scale. Its becoming fashionable. The experimental city is about to become one of the idea that everybody
knows about, thinks about; and a few actually do it, make it
happen......Whatever it is that decides when such changes in
fashion, in culture, come about - I'd say that is the real
futurology, the thing to try to predict......But I dont believe
in prediction at that scale, the scale of history, you might
say. I dont believe that this city of ours was pre-ordained,
or was entirely a function of the recent past. It need not
have happened. And we two might not have been here now, trying
to set it going. But I'm glad we are, Utopia. I'll never forget
this. Our moment. Or one of them. I can't believe its really
happening.

Utopia: I dont know what to say. No need to say anything, I
guess. More coffee?

Numeroso: OK. What are we doing, do you think - trying to
improve life, or just enjoying it?

Utopia: Well I'm pretty sure we're doing both. It took a lot

of effort by some strongly motivated people to get to this point.
But now that the experiment seems bound to happen, one way or
another, its becoming part of life, something to enjoy, if one
can, or to suffer, if things go wrong. The whole thing could
go very wrong. I expect you've thought of that.

Numeroso: No I hadn't. So far I've not given it much thought.
I came because I was asked. And to be with you. You know that.
But I suppose you're right - we could have some sleepless nights.
What happens if the people living here get violent? If they
start killing each other. Is that on the cards, or has Unesco
got some rules that he is going to enforce after all?

Utopia: That's for us to decide. He said its to be as realistic as we dare to make it. He'll accept what we say.

Numeroso: Perhaps he will, but if I was one of the people
coming to live here I'd want some kind of security I think......
or would I? This sounds like the most difficult question we
have to decide. If the thing's to be more than a game there'll
have to be some real risks. But I'm forgetting. Its to be a
semi-fiction. When it gets too dangerous it will be a matter
of simulating what's supposed to happen so that it looks real to
the tv audience, but not to those involved. But what about its
political effect, on the viewers? Are there any limits there?

Utopia: No. This is to be one bit of tv where the only censor
is to be the channel selecter. Unesco is going to beam it world-
wide from sattelites. Of course, with the present technology,
each country can decide for itself whether to re-transmit on
their own networks, but there'll be videotapes too which will
reach some people, at least, in most countries. But its not our
job to think about that, its outside our influence. Its up to
us to make it as perfect as possible. To give the future a
chance.

Numeroso smiles.

Utopia: Shall we go outside? Its getting hot in the van.

Numeroso: You're quite fragile, aren't you, when it comes to
realities. Yes. Lets go outside. Its a beautiful morning.
Its perfect.

332

Next day. Unesco arrives. The conversation continues.

Unesco: Don't let me interrupt. I'm only here to listen. There's a meeting tomorrow and I have to make a report.

Utopia: Perhaps you'd like a summary of our thinking so far? We've discussed a lot of possibilities and it would help us both, I think, to describe them in brief, and to hear what you think. We could be losing sight of the goal.

Unesco: The goal, Utopia? I remember you lecturing about goals. You said that fixed goals are over: things of the industrial past. If the process is informative we should be open to act on what it teaches. Isn't that what you said? Or somebody did.[3]

Utopia: Yes of course. I should have said 'we can learn from your reactions'. But its hard to shed that reductionist jargon, the vocabulary of the narrow path.

Unesco: That's a nice way to put it. But I don't pay so much attention to the words people us. I listen more to the tone of voice.

Numeroso: Before we go on, Unesco, could you tell us what you really had in mind when you proposed this experiment?

Unesco: Yes of course. I had two very clear reasons. Firstly, I am tired of hearing from experts that so many of the world's problems are insoluble: poverty, malnutrition, pollution, road accidents, bureaucracy, illiteracy, inflation......there are literally hundreds of such problems, and most of them getting worse. So why not make a fresh start? Try to clear our minds, to rethink the possibilities in a less restricted context? The conventional planning methods seem to be too limiting to make real difference. And my second reason is that I've come to doubt the futurologists, the people in the think tanks. Too much thinking and too little practice. They seem to forget that technology is not just an idea: its action. Its the making of physical changes to the world, its altering nature, to an extent at least. And such changes, such actions, create a re-action. A social reaction, when we see for ourselves what the changed world is really like. Seeing it, and ex- periencing it, changes our perceptions. I'm sure of that. It tells you things you didn't know about yourself and leads you to act in new ways. Ways that are not predictable from a

theoretical model, or concept.[4] That's my belief. That's why
you're here. Ideas are essential to generate something new.
But I don't believe that they can predict its effects. That's
my theory!

Utopia: That's not a theory, Unesco. Its a morality, an ethic.
A theory is meant to predict. To control. To create certainty.
But what you're saying is that ideas, if acted upon, do the opposite. Your belief, as I understand it, is that we should
accept not knowing what the future will be like and that we
should trust in the abilities of ourselves, and of everyone else,
to be surprised by what happens, to be changed by it, and to be
able to react in new ways that at present we do not know? To
seek to fix the future into a predicted form is, by this ethic
of yours, a wrong thing to do. Its to deny us our humantiy, our
ability to be.[5] Life will change beyond our expectations.[6]

Numeroso is silent. He looks surprised. A little embarassed,
perhaps. Its getting dark. The scribe knows that they have a
lot more to say and wonders how it is to be fitted into 3000
words. Most of them are gone.

Numeroso: Its time we spoke of the details, the kinds of new
technology to be tested in the city and the precise questions
that the experiment is meant to answer. But what we've just
been saying makes me ask if even that is going too far. Its
hard to see how to begin with enough reality to generate action
while leaving space for genuine doubt.

Unesco: What specific proposals have you discussed?

Numeroso: Many. Here are a few. Not in any special order but
just as I remember them. Education: very largely without books,
perhaps without literacy, even. The paperless office. No jobs.
Everything is to be produced automatically, without workers or
managements, or else is made by hand by those who need it. No
cash, just credit cards, and a guaranteed unearned income. At
first all structures will be temporary - mobile homes and the
like. Public access to all information, personal files included,
no copyrights, no privacy of information, public or private.
Each profession is given the task of translating its specialised
services into a mixture of computer aids and do-it-yourself.

334

Private cars and buses to be replaced by automated minicars
and minibuses accessible by credit card, and free of accidents,
congestion, and parking problems, being computer controlled.
Walking and cycling facilities to have top priority in city
design. Private ownership of space to be limited to the times
when the persons concerned are actually present, each person's
territory being a mobile entity in law. Law-making, and law-
changing, being a public responsibility to which everyone has to
give a lot of time. Referenda, by tv viewdata systems, every
day. Have I said enough to let you see what we have in mind?
Obviously its going to call for very different motivations, and
ways of living, than those we are used to. To discover those is,
I imagine, the main question.

Unesco: All this sounds like technology and western culture
carried to the extreme. What about the poor countries?

Utopia: We propose that it begins, as you say, with the most
advanced technologies we know, but with a new factor that changes
the picture completely: negative growth, or rather planned
economic decline. The aim of the imaginary economy is to
gradually approach the levels of income that are common in the
majority of the world, a fraction of western incomes now. Why
not try to close the gap from the top down? That's the idea
we'd most like to see tried. Why not? Its no more astonishing
than was the growth of industrialisation in the first place.
The alternative technology people have in many cases shown the
way.

Numeroso: You dont have to argue with us, Utopia. We agree I'm
sure. But, where its a proposal that seems to call for per-
suasion, shouldn't we be thinking of letting the inhabitants
of the city decide for themselves? I don't think I understand
the politics of this experiment. Who's in control?

At this point my story becomes the introductory scene of a
fiction which could be continued.

References to the real world:

1. Jones, J. Christopher, "Trying to Design the Future", Design,

September 1967, <u>225</u>, page 35 ff.

2. Paulo Soleri is the architect and initiator of the ecological
   micro-city Arcosanti in the desert north of Phoenix, Arizona,
   USA.

3. Jones, J. Christopher, <u>Design Methods, 1980 Edition</u>, (New
   York, Toronto, Chichester, Brisbane, John Wiley & Sons, 1981),
   page xxii.

4. As I was typing this I switched on the radio to hear the
   voice of my friend, J.K. Page, speaking the second reason in
   a broadcast for the Open University course T101, Living With
   Technology. (Open University, Milton Keynes, Bucks, Britain)

5. Heidegger, Martin, "The Question Concerning Technology", in
   <u>Martin Heidegger, Basic Writings</u>, edited by David Farrel
   Krell, (London and Henley, Routledge & Kegan Paul, 1978),
   pages 284 to 317, and throughout the book.

6. I was visiting Welsh villages, asking people to write their
   impressions of how they expect their village to be in the
   future. Mrs Clarice Mary Allen, of Llanwrtyd Wells, wrote
   "I think it will be changed beyond any expectations.". I
   dont think I have ever read a more intelligent comment
   on the future. Quoted from <u>25 Views of Wales</u>, edited by
   Jones, J. Christopher, (London, Jones Family Editions, 1980).